Shits and Giggles - Diaries of a Solo Mom

Single Mom, Strong Mom

By
Monya Maxwell

© 2024 Monya Maxwell

All rights reserved.

No part of this book may be reproduced, distributed, or transmitted in any form or by any means, including photocopying, recording, or other electronic or mechanical methods, without the prior written permission of the publisher, except in the case of brief quotations embodied in critical reviews and certain other noncommercial uses permitted by copyright law.

ISBN: 978-0-7961-9317-9

First Edition: June 2024

Published by Monya Maxwell

Disclaimer: This is a work of nonfiction. The events and experiences described in this book are true to the best of the author's memory. Some names and identifying details have been changed to protect the privacy of individuals.

This book is dedicated to my children.
All I want for you is to have the best possible life,
and most of all...to be happy!

Index

Introduction 1
The Story of a Single-Solo Mom 5
How Do You Do It? 11
The Cheeky Mouths of Babes 18
Let's Talk About Income 25
Living on a Tight Budget 32
Financial Abuse 38
The Rules and Expectations 44
Society's View 51
The Single-Mom's Burden on Society 56
The Effect of Stigmas and Stereotypes on Children ... 62
The Maslow Hierarchy 70
Medical Emergencies 80
Single, NOT Ready to Mingle 85
Ready to Date Again? 92
Lessons Learned 108
In Closing 115
References 118
Other Books Mentioned in this Book 121
About the Author 122

Introduction

'Shits and Giggles - Diaries of a Solo Mom' is not just a book; it's a journey through the trials and triumphs of single motherhood. This book is a collection of my life experiences, insights, research and the lessons I've learned. It's raw, honest, and sometimes downright hilarious.

These past six years have been tough, the toughest I have ever faced. Often I thought, 'This is it; it is breaking me.' But somehow, I always get back up and push forward. I'm repeatedly unsure where the strength comes from, but I look at my children and say, 'I have to try again.' Without them, I don't know where I would be today. Perhaps I'd wander the world, begging for supplies and rides, not knowing what tomorrow would bring. Look at Maslow's hierarchy of motivation, explained later in this book and then perhaps this statement might not sound so out of place.

From the day we are born, our lives start taking shape, and our brains begin creating patterns based on environmental influences. If a baby cries, the mom attends to it. If a toddler hugs his dad's leg, he picks the child up. And so on. Things in our lives go right, and things in our lives go wrong.

We have no control over many things, but one thing I got right is accepting things for what they are. Life is far from perfect. I am not a perfect parent, neither were my parents or any other parents, if I may be so bold to say it. But I try to be the parent for my children that I wish I'd had. In this, I am just trying to be the best version of myself. After all, I am human, just like the parents who raised me, or the people who were in the shopping line with me earlier today, or those who travelled the same roads as I. And, as much as I know about what I do wrong, I am also aware of what I do right.

The trick is to be kind to yourself as a parent and accept when you are wrong. Apologise and try to do better next time. Raising children can be challenging in moments, and I think the world is becoming more complex for each new generation. In all honesty, our blueprints are outdated. Considering this, it is impossible to be a perfect parent or human. And this makes single parenting even harder. Or so I think, considering I do not have a time travel machine to see what happened decades ago to compare single paring from the past to the present.

So many nights I have spent sitting on the bathroom floor crying to the point that my tear ducts dried out. Yes, the tears would not flow anymore. Dry tears - when you know you cried them all out. The same heartbreaking emotions of defeat, regret, and sometimes even anger, accompanied by dry tears. Raising children, we get to meet the true nature of ourselves as children test us in ways no one else has before!

I also believe it is impossible to truly know love until you hold your first child in your arms! That moment and the moments to follow change you. And with all the difficulties and challenges, there are those memorable moments of things your children said that were so funny or completely out of place, or when they dressed themselves and their clothes were the wrong way around. These memories are so special and make all the difficult moments so worth it.

In writing this book, I am opening myself up, sharing hard truths and realities, and being immensely vulnerable. And I will probably offend some people. But I hope this book may give comfort and inspiration to others going through similar situations and perhaps provide a different perspective for society on what goes on behind the closed doors of a single mom's house. I hope my story can inspire others to change, grow personally, and emerge from challenging circumstances. Change is not always easy, but can be achieved through determination.

Single moms have to fill every role in one house. It is a big responsibility, and many single moms do not have great support systems. As difficult as some days may be, we get up every day and do it for our children, putting one foot in front of the other.

In this book, I speak hard truths and discuss stigmas, and it might not be easy for everyone to digest. I also generalise throughout the book. Please do not get offended – the simple old saying 'If the shoe fits, wear it'. If it does not fit, put it back down.

So why did I decide to write this book? And it does feel like a taboo topic to discuss as we have unconsciously become accustomed to social norms. Last year, I moved from one side of Johannesburg to another. I was going through the process to view properties to rent. During this process, I struggled to find a place to rent, to the point it caused a delay in my moving plans. At first, I could not figure it out. At this point, I was still very oblivious to the 'single mom' stigmas. I thought people were weird when there were odd comments or people behaved in a way I could not understand. With the frustration of doors being shut when I was only trying to schedule a viewing appointment, I found out many people do not want to rent to single mothers. And I do understand why, as so many struggle financially and become a liability. This then got me thinking, what else is held against us? And it seems society is well aware that a lot, actually most, separated fathers do not pay child maintenance. Fucking pathetic!

I am also from a Western South African culture, and things are different in different cultures. Just keep this in mind. During my photography years, I have had the pleasure of meeting many different people from different cultures and have seen how some cultures are open and supportive towards single mothers. And sadly how in other cultures it seems to be a shame. My aim for this book is to speak up and shed light on some of the challenges single mothers face daily and explain things from our perspective. We try to blend into society, yet our circumstances are very different. Like any mother, we want what is best for our children, and we fight the good fight for them every day. Even though we get worn out, we too only want what is best for them.

I speak about my children in the book, by name and thus changed their names for obvious reasons.

The Story of a Single-Solo Mom

I remember the day I found out I was pregnant. It was a mix of emotions—excitement, fear, and a sense of wonder. I had no idea what was in store for me, but I knew one thing: my life was changing forever.

Let me introduce myself. I am Monya, a mother of two beautiful, bright children and a photographer. Oh, and I almost forgot to mention, I am a single mother. Perhaps I omitted that part intentionally. That label 'single mom'- I am so weary of it. At this point, I aspire to be a thriving single mother, or better yet, a progressing person. I long to walk the streets as any other woman and mother, without labels or waves of shame (shame bestowed on me by societal stereotypes and stigmas).

Allow me to explain my frustration with the 'single mom' concept. Whether it's the 'struggling single mom' or just the 'single mom,' the label is often accompanied by phrases like 'Gosh, you have your hands full. Poor thing,' or 'How do you manage?' The thing that gets me the most is the insinuation that a 'single mom's' children are always the naughty and out-of-control ones. According to several studies, children of single mothers are also unfairly perceived as less intelligent. Just stupid – pun, no pun...

Being a 'single mom' is not a disease. People may pity you, but they also keep their distance, fearing they might catch the 'single mom disease.' Or worse yet, fearing that the 'single mom' might steal their 'hus-bank,' or was that 'husband'? Okay, perhaps a bit cheeky of me. I only hope to change the stigma surrounding the 'single mom' label, shed some light on it, and share my frustrations and insights.

I prefer to refer to myself as a mother. Yes, I am raising my children alone. And yes, there are challenges. We all have our struggles. Let's acknowledge this for a moment. I believe it also has a lot to do with one's approach. There are some upsides to doing it alone. For example, when you leave a toxic relationship, there is more space for yourself in your relationship with yourself, than there was before. However, there are downsides as well, as humans naturally crave companionship. There are days when you are tired and lack the patience to deal with a homework project issue, or when you have too many tasks and too few hours in a day – when you purely need 36-hour days to get through. Or when your child is sick the week you have deadlines and are so busy at work – not the week before when all was quiet.

There is no right or wrong between single-parent or dual-parent households or couples who split up and manage to co-parent successfully. I must admit I am envious of those who get it right. They are few but admirable. You set an example for many who can only wish to do the same. In the case of a split family (whether divorce or breakup), the ideal situation is a healthy household and making the most of the path one is on. Do I wish for my children to have a healthy two-parent household or two separate stable households? Of course, I do. But that was not the way things worked out. I never intended to get married to get divorced. Sometimes life just does not turn out as you hoped and wished for. But you adjust and accept the path ahead.

So, where did things go wrong, if I dare ask such a simple question?

My childhood foundations were laid somewhat skewed, creating a flawed framework. This led to several dysfunctional friendships, work environments, and ultimately, romantic relationships. One thing led to another, and then one day, it was like a brick hit me square in the face. I found myself asking, 'What the hell just happened? How did I get here?'

There are parts of the story I will share and parts that are not for me to tell. What unfolded in my life affected several different people. Some call me crazy, and perhaps I am. Or it's their way to control the gossip and protect their reputation. Or I am just crazy – I do not think I have met a crazy person to compare with, and in today's world, this term is used so loosely that it can have a different meaning depending on the context it is used in. Sometimes it could even be used as a compliment 'It is crazy how you figured the problem out', or 'It is crazy phenomenal new flavours!'. Okay, enough with the crazy talk, let's move on. It is up to you to decide what you define as 'crazy.'

Wait, hang on! I had to Google it. Call me crazy or obsessed with facts. I searched Google for the term 'meaning of crazy,' and this is what came up:

(adjective) Mad, especially as manifested in wild or aggressive behaviour.

(adjective) Extremely enthusiastic.

(adverb) Extremely.

(noun) A mad person.

You decide what the word 'crazy' means to you when you use it. Hopefully, it is not a word you use often to label another person or in everyday conversations. Labelling people is not nice. A cup of tea, however, is nice. And you get so many different flavours today. I might switch completely from coffee to tea...uhm. Maybe not. I still enjoy my two cups of coffee per day. But hibiscus tea...that one I tried and will gladly give it a skip. The other tea flavours with peach or ginger and chilli - are simply delicious!

Did I ever dream of becoming a single solo mom? No, of course not. I was raised naïve, as daddy's little girl. In my dad's eyes, I could do nothing wrong. In my mother's eyes, I could do nothing right. My Oupa (grandfather) used to tease me and say: 'Monya, you are always in shit, it is just the depth that differs.' That was pretty much my childhood. On one side of life, I was scared of witches. And on the other side, I dreamed of fairy tales. So yes, like most girls, I wanted a fairy tale life where things were pretty and magical and smelled like roses with nothing to worry about. But I always looked over my shoulder, anticipating the fairy tale to become a nightmare. Life shook me around a few times, and I had to wake up from the fairy tale dream, to find myself trapped in a nightmare. But going through all that, I found my feet, in normal life with its ups and downs.

Raising children is a significant responsibility, whether you go at it alone or not. For the rest of our lives, we are responsible for these little humans, who grow up way too fast, thinking they know everything at the mere age of ten years. Oh, my gosh! The mouth they come with these days. If mom does not know the answer, well, then she must Google it – 'Just Google it, Mom!' Doing it alone is difficult and presents extra challenges, but so many of us do it and, in the process, form strong bonds with our children. With strength and resilience, we endure the task at hand.

Life as a single-solo mom has its quirks and challenges. One of the most amusing parts, if I can call it that, is the realisation that you have become the master of all trades. Need a plumber? I'm your girl. Need a chef? Checked off (as long as it doesn't contain any vegetables, my children hate it - ugh)! Need a mediator in sibling disputes (and this area is a huge challenge because I grew up as an only child. This shit is foreign to me)? I've got it covered, or at least try my best. It's like being a superhero, but instead of fighting villains, you are fighting household chores and parenting dilemmas.

One of the biggest challenges of being a single-solo mom is finding time for yourself. It's easy to get caught up in the daily grind of work, chores, and parenting, but it's important to carve out some time for self-care. Whether it's a relaxing bath, a walk in the park, or just a few moments of quiet reflection, taking care of yourself is essential to take care of others.

Another challenge is dealing with societal expectations and stereotypes. There's a misconception that single moms are somehow less capable or less deserving of respect than mothers in traditional family structures. But the truth is, single moms are some of the strongest, most resilient people you'll ever meet. We juggle work, parenting, and household responsibilities with grace and determination, and we deserve to be celebrated for our strength and perseverance. We are one person doing a two-person job.

Despite the challenges, being a single-solo mom is also incredibly rewarding. There's a special bond that forms between a single mom and her children, a bond that is forged through shared experiences and mutual support. Watching my children grow and thrive, knowing that I played a role in shaping their lives, is the greatest reward of all.

While you are reading this book, I hope to shed light on the realities of single motherhood, challenge stereotypes and stigmas, and inspire other single moms to embrace their strength and resilience. We may be raising our children alone, but we are far from alone in our journey. Together, we can change the narrative surrounding single motherhood and show the world just how astounding single moms truly are, and we are just like any other woman.

How Do You Do It?

How do I do it? I don't know. How do you take a bar of soap out of its packaging? You just do it. You put one foot before the other and get on with the moves. Some days are better and easier than others, while others are horrid. When it's easy, we get on with the day, pump the music and dance to the beat. We look forward to bedtime when we can crash and rest our weary souls. But on those horrid days, oh boy, they are tough. You need an extra bit of strength, and you dig deep to find it. You rely on that inner voice that says, 'You can do this.'

Often, I hide my troubles. I don't want people to know when things are tough or when I am down and out. I put up this façade and pretend to be okay when things might not be all that 'okay'. People often ask me, 'How do you do it all?' My answer is usually a smile and a shrug. The truth is, there's no secret formula or magic trick. It's about survival, determination, and love. It's about knowing that giving up is not an option because little lives depend on you.

The truth is, being a single mom is hard as hell! I can't lie about it. You are the nurturer and the provider. You must be the mom and the dad, the good cop and the bad cop. You must be it all! The teacher, protector, doctor, and still try to figure out how to fix the bike. And through all this, still find the time to somehow care for yourself in between all the chaos. I think it has a lot to do with mindset, to be able to have a growth mindset (more to be discussed later). Accepting things for what they are, even if it is chaos. One of the key things that help me manage is prioritising. I've learned to focus on what's truly important and let go of the rest. Does the house need to be spotless every day? No. Do I need to be there for my children when they need me? Absolutely. It's a balancing act, and it's not always perfect, but it works for us. It is what it is.

Secondly, I would say, that knowing and accepting you are not perfect. And NO ONE is perfect. They just put their best photos and smiles on Facebook and Instagram. That, in itself, can be a facade. So, don't get caught up with it and compare yourself to the other families out there who seem so perfect.

And then third, I had to learn to be kind to myself. I don't always get it right, and some days I lose my cool and shout. There have been many times that I went to my children and apologised for behaving wrongly or shouting before they could explain the situation, which then turned out to have a very reasonable explanation. And there was no need to shout in the first place. But in essence, because you must fill every role and stress builds up, it can get to a point where you just lose your cool completely.

But you put yourself back together, and in the quiet of night, you ponder how you can do it better or what different approach can I take. But I guess most mothers feel this way – single or not.

Giving yourself time out is not a bad thing. My bathroom has become my holy place where I hide, cry in private, or sit and give myself a serious pep talk to get my act together, to line up the ducks. Support systems are invaluable. I've built a network of friends, and other single parents who understand what I'm going through. We support each other, share advice, and sometimes merely listen. Knowing that I'm not alone in this journey makes a huge difference.

Being a single mom does not mean you are an alien. Okay, some days I forget to put on deodorant or do not take time to fix my hair, and I look like I climbed out of the laundry basket. But it's okay. I am still human, and not an alien (or are we the aliens?).

My children go to the same school as others, we drive the same streets as others and go to the same shops as others. I smile, laugh, and cry, just like other moms. I have to deal with the same problems of siblings fighting in the car or when they do not feel like doing homework, or taking what feels like forever to get out of the bath. And that after taking an hour of death threats just to get them in the damn bath, in the first place!

As mentioned before, I grew up as an only child. There were no siblings to compete with, and the bathroom most times was mine alone. So, my parents did not mind if I bathed for an hour. They got to watch their television soapies (old-time soap operas) in peace while I was slipping and sliding in the tub.

This sibling thing, where they go from best friends to hating each other with all the yelling and toys being thrown at each other or bedroom doors being slammed, can be a lot to deal with! And all this plays out in seconds! And then a few minutes later they are playing again like nothing happened. This boggles my mind! Like, what on earth? Am I raising two aliens (aliens again)? After ten years of parenting, I am still grinding to get used to the sibling fights.

Raising children is not easy, no matter who you are. It takes stamina! When they come to you with a real meaningful 'I am sorry, Mom' and hug you, it all melts away. All the chaos, all the dysfunction, in that moment, just melts away. And those little random 'I love you, Mom' moments are priceless!

This reminds me of a moment of a failed time-out attempt. My children were playing outside on the lawn, right by the door and close enough for me to keep an eye on them while I was busy preparing supper in the kitchen. Now, I don't quite recall their ages, but I think Abby was about four and Dean about two. Abby did something naughty; I think she hit her brother, or they fought over a toy or something. So, I reprimanded her and told her to have a few minutes' time-out at the steps (back when we thought time-out was still a good thing to do). Dean then looks at this and realises he is now alone outside and that is no fun. He then decides to go and sit next to Abby in time-out, and just like that, going from enemies to besties in seconds, they start playing in the time-out corner.

I am trying to get dinner done and need the energy to handle this situation. Reprimands go from one to the other, trying to separate them in their time-out corners. At one point, I tried having them sit with their backs towards each other in the hopes this would not lead to more playfulness. And then I tried separating them on different steps further apart. But alas, this turns into chaos. Every time things just ended up in giggles because time-out has now become a challenging game because they teamed up against Mom. In the end, I chased them both back outside to go play, where they celebrated their victory. This whole dilemma played out in about a ten-minute timeframe or less.

Kids! 'Have kids they said. It will be fun!'. A saying I heard somewhere and always laugh when I say it out loud.

Routine is another crucial element. Having a set schedule helps keep things running smoothly. Then children know what to expect, and it creates a sense of stability and predictability in their lives. Mornings start with the usual hustle of getting everyone ready for school and work. Breakfast is quick, usually a bowl of cereal and making up beds, and then we're out the door. The school run is a mix of last-minute checks in the hopes everyone brushed their teeth and packed a water bottle. Evenings are another story, doing homework and unpacking bags. Dinner time is chaotic but also the time we come together as a family. It's a small window of calm amidst the storm of daily life. One of the best things about our routines is the bedtime ritual. After dinner, we wind down with some quiet time. Each child has a dedicated book reading time where I read to them - bedtime stories are a must! Each night (okay, no. More accurately would be most nights), we pick a book and dive into a different world. It's a comforting way to end the day and helps the children settle down for the night.

But let's be honest, not every day goes as planned. There are days when we oversleep, and we're running late from the get-go and tempers are short. Sometimes I attend sports games, and sometimes I miss them. Occasionally, I pick them up from school on time, while other times I'm a bit late – 'a bit late' is perhaps understated as there have been times I was super late! However, we always discuss things, and they wait for me, even if I'm late. And when I am late, I explain why to prevent any panic or added stress.

Of course, there are days when the routine goes out the window, and that's okay too. Flexibility is essential. We adapt and move on. As a single mom, finding the balance between work, parenting, and personal time can be a real juggling act. But with a sense of humour and a lot of love, every day becomes an adventure. The challenges may be tough, but the rewards are immeasurable. I've learned to go with the flow and not stress over the small stuff. Spilled milk can be cleaned up, and a missing jacket needs to be dealt with.

Despite the predictability of routines, life has its surprises. There are unexpected school projects, sudden illnesses, and unplanned events that throw a wrench in our plans. When these disruptions occur, I remind myself that it's okay to deviate from the plan. Flexibility and resilience are key to navigating these challenges. Our weekends are a blend of structure and spontaneity. We have a loose plan but leave room for impromptu adventures. Sometimes we visit the park, other times we stay in and have a movie or series marathon. These moments of freedom are essential for recharging and reconnecting as a family.

Self-care is not a luxury; it's a necessity. I've learned that taking care of myself is crucial to being able to take care of my children. Whether it's a few minutes of meditation, a good book, or a bubble bath, these small acts of self-care recharge my batteries and keep me going. I tend to reserve my alone time for the mornings, like going for a run or enjoying the occasional breakfast. Then, I often wind up working late at night, once they are in bed. My hours aren't structured around the typical traditional office hours if we can call them that. I just 'wing' it most days and see what I need to get done for the day and what time of day would be best suited for each task. My hours are personalised to work within our little household's bounds.

Despite the challenges, the moments of pure joy make it all worthwhile. The laughter of my children, their hugs, and the pride I feel watching them grow and thrive are priceless. These moments remind me why I do what I do and give me the strength to keep going.

In conclusion, how do I do it? By taking it one day at a time, embracing the chaos, and focusing on the love that binds us together. Routine and chaos coexist in our lives. It's this balance that keeps us grounded and allows us to navigate the ups and downs of life. It's not always easy, but it's my journey, and I wouldn't trade it for anything.

The Cheeky Mouths of Babes

I often joke that my mother had only one of me, but I have two of me to deal with. I was a cheeky little girl at times. But we were also raised in a time when children were seen and not heard. If you were out of line, you got a spanking back into yesterday to fetch your attitude you left behind – as if our parents thought we could time travel. As cheeky as I could be at times, I was also too afraid to speak my mind. However, today's children get to be cheeky. Gosh, and do they know just how to do it? Children have a way of saying the most unexpected things. Their innocence and honesty often lead to hilarious and sometimes profound statements that leave us adults speechless. I've had my fair share of these moments, and they never fail to bring a smile to my face.

One afternoon, my daughter was about one and a half years old. I don't quite recall what started the argument between her and me. And I reprimanded her for her behaviour, in the end asking her, 'Where are your manners?'. Now, I'm not quite sure what response I expected from a one-and-a-half-year-old girl at the time; perhaps it was meant as a rhetorical question. But she looks at me, rubs her chin with one hand, with her other hand on her hip, and then points over her shoulder with the hand that rubbed her chin and says, 'Outside!'. Followed by a long pause moment in which she tried to see if her answer was correct. Honestly, I cannot be sure what her thought pattern was at the time but it was clear she did not know what the word 'manners' meant – considering her age and she was still increasing her vocabulary. Well, I burst out laughing, and whatever the reason for the discipline was, was defeated because she won with her little cheeky answer and smile.

There was a time when my son, the youngest, had a thing for sleeping with his new shoes when he was a toddler. I have a video where I recorded an argument with him before bedtime, asking him to please take his shoes off and get into bed. Both my children have very strong wills, and as beautiful as it can be, it can also be infuriating when you need to negotiate with 'terrorists'. Often I would joke with clients and say 'Politicians did not invent bribery and corruption. Toddlers did!'. My son would end up going to bed wearing his new shoes! After waiting at least an hour or more to make sure he was fast asleep, I would then go into their room (they were sharing at the time) to remove his shoes and place them next to his bed. He went through a phase where he was fascinated with new shoes and still is today.

Abby, at one stage, went through a phase of asking the strangest questions at the oddest of times. Like, while I was driving, she would ask me, 'Mom, how long does brain surgery take?'. What? How the heck must I know? I am a photographer, not a brain surgeon or any surgeon for that matter. And if I explain we need to look it up on the internet, she would just tune me straight out to ask Google while I am driving (which I still do not have voice activation active on my phone). Their questions can also be deeply philosophical. Other questions I would get asked are things like how many types of sharks are there, or how big are whales. I sit there wondering, where on earth does she come up with these questions? Was it something at school? No, she would say, she was just wondering. Okay, my girl. Keep dreaming in wonder.

Children have magnificent little brains. It is astounding to watch how they develop and how their brains perceive the world, trying to make sense of things. They are growing up in a beautiful but also complex time in history. My two children are fascinated with the concept that I did not have a cell phone when I was their age. The look of shock and horror on Abby's face when I told her I did not have a mobile phone because it was not yet invented. In a failed attempt to counter it, I announced we did have Lego (I don't want to come across as ancient) or played with washed mango pips, which we turned into a doll by drawing a face on it (I hope I am not the only weird child here who had one of those). But she was still jaw-droppingly trying to comprehend that her mother is older than mobile phone technology. 'How old are you, Mom? Are you ancient?' Gee, thanks, my girl, I thought.

And this brings me to another point. Children also have an uncanny ability to blurt out the truth, even when it's embarrassing. Many other moms have experienced the same. You know, children just love to announce how old they are, and they always look forward to their birthdays, for the gifts and parties but also to being one year older. Just one. And how they would also go into detail to say 'I am four and a half years old'. That half year is important! BUT, they do not quite comprehend that a mom does not like to announce her age. So, they would walk up to strangers in a park or have a conversation in the shopping line and tell people, 'This is my mom, and she is 40 years old!'. Like what the heck. Ya, tell everyone who your mom is, but my age does not need to be public knowledge, and it is not relevant information. I often felt so embarrassed and took me months to convince them to stop doing it. At first, they thought it was normal and important information to strike up a conversation and to share. To them, it was like telling someone your name and that you are a girl – state the obvious. I pleaded with them to stop, instead, it became a game to them thinking it was the funniest thing ever! Months! It took months, might even have been a year before they stopped doing it.

Humour is an essential part of our family dynamic. We laugh a lot, and these cheeky comments from my children provide endless entertainment. They also serve as a reminder not to take life too seriously. In the grand scheme of things, it's the laughter and joy we share that matter most.

Oh, and when Abby was still a small toddler, I quickly had to learn to stop cursing in the car. You know those road rage moments when someone steals your parking space, the one you were waiting for a minute (which felt like a lifetime as you envision you could have been inside the store with your trolley already) or when someone cuts you off at the stop? Yes, those silly moments, and then you say something, not thinking your two-year-old is paying attention. Well, they hear far more than what we give them credit for. Someone cut me off in the parking while trying to exit, and I had to slam the brakes. Okay, we were in a parking driving like 5-10km per hour. So nothing majorly fast or dangerous. At that moment I said 'Fokkit'. This is Afrikaans and translates to 'fuck it'. For weeks after that, when I hit the brakes just a little too hard, even at a normal stop, Abby would shout from the back 'Fokkit'. I had to come up with another word just to say every time I stopped to try and reprogram her vocabulary. For long after that, I had to be careful with what I said in front of her. She hears everything!

Oh, how I miss those days when my children liked to clean – yip the broom and vacuum were Dean's favourite toys at the time. When Dean was just over one year old, he had an absolute fascination with brooms and the vacuum cleaner pipe. We lived in a complex with a communal garden, and each unit had a little patio. Most people would leave their mops and brooms in the corner of their patio. Dean was so funny. Leave him outside for too long, and we would end up with a collection of brooms on our patio. I got to the point where I knew exactly which broom belonged to which unit. Neighbours found it quite funny.

I must say, at the time I was still married to my children 's father, and writing about this incident now, I wonder if the neighbours would still have found it funny if I was a single mother. Or would my children have been labelled as naughty or unruly?

These moments, while sometimes challenging, are a precious part of parenting. They offer opportunities to teach, to learn, and to connect with my children on a deeper level. One year, when my children were still very young, I asked them what they would like for Christmas. Abby wanted a real unicorn and Dean a real dinosaur—not toys—real ones. This was a challenging time when their imaginations were so raw and developing, while they were also technically dealing with the divorce and having a stepmother they were told to call 'mom.' During this time, which is normal for their age, children cannot always distinguish between fantasy and reality.

Added to the stress of a divorce were two households that could not agree on anything and a child who thought his birth mother was going to die because he now needed to call his new stepmother 'mom.' Keeping this and other factors in mind (without discussing any more of the mess from the divorce), I decided to be honest with them and explain that unicorns and dinosaurs are not real. Unicorns are fantasy animals, and dinosaurs are extinct. They took this quite easily and happily settled for toys instead on their wish list. But soon after that, we had to talk about Father Christmas and the Tooth Fairy as well. How do I now lie and tell them Father Christmas and the Tooth Fairy is real?

Other people got very upset with me and started telling me how I should raise my children and how dare I spoil this for them. It was a full-blown attack without anyone even asking me why I chose to do this. And yes, many families enjoy these stories. But keep in mind if your child is going through trauma at the time, they often resort to fantasy to deal with it. I did not try to spoil fantasy for my children. I tried to create a bridge so they could, to some extent and age-appropriately, distinguish between reality and fantasy. I still, today, encourage them to be creative and dream things up. If we cannot imagine it, we cannot invent it. Dean is busy inventing his flying car and has named it... a few times... each time something different. And this car has an ATM on board... go figure.

To end the chapter on a lighter note. I still recall Abby's first day of grade one. It was a busy morning, as it normally is with lots of excited parents taking their children either back to school, or for their first day of Grade one. There was no parking available close to the school entrance, so we had to park a bit further away. Walking from the car, all dressed up and proud in her school uniform and rolling her wheely school bag, we held hands. As we approach the gate, she tells me I can let go of her hand because she is a big girl now. Gosh, my heart melted!

In conclusion, the cheeky mouths of babes are a source of endless amusement and unexpected wisdom. Their unfiltered honesty and imaginative declarations keep life interesting and full of laughter. As a parent, I cherish these moments, knowing they are fleeting but immensely valuable.

Let's Talk About Income

Income is a topic that often feels taboo, especially in the context of single parenting. But it's an essential part of life that we need to address openly and honestly. As a single mom, managing income can be incredibly challenging, and it requires careful planning and budgeting. It's about making smart choices and sometimes sacrifices to ensure my children have what they need.

When I first became a single mom, I was overwhelmed by the financial responsibilities. There were days when I worried about how I would pay the important bills like rent and provide the essentials for my children. It was a stressful time, but it also taught me valuable lessons about money management and resilience. Budgeting became my lifeline. I learned to track every cent and make every rand count. I created a detailed budget that accounted for all our expenses, from rent and utilities to groceries and school supplies. It wasn't easy, but it was necessary. Budgeting helped me prioritise our needs and cut out unnecessary expenses. And yes, I understand when there are no unnecessary expenses left to cut and still not enough to cover the bills.

In these cases also explored other ways to save money. Shopping sales, signing up for loyalty programs, and buying in bulk became part of my routine. I found that small savings added up over time, making a significant difference in our budget. At one point, my savings accounts were empty. Embarrassingly, I even had to use all the savings I had built up over a while for my children , just to get food and toiletries in the house and to clothe them. Sometimes when life knocks you, it really knocks you down. It floors you! And like any business, there are seasons when business is thriving and slow seasons.

Have you ever felt stuck? Not physically stuck, but when life keeps tossing you around from one end to the other, and you're left wondering what the heck is going on? Is there a purpose to everything that happens to us, or a lesson to be learned? What the heck is going on here? Can things go this wrong? It's hard to have faith. To me, it feels like the word faith has become like a band-aid. When things go wrong, we try to have faith, we beg in our prayers for God's mercy, help, or answers. I'm still not sure what exactly it means to have faith, but prayer is what we do when we feel like we have nothing left.

Photography is my main income stream. I turned to my passion for photography long before the divorce and started offering my services to friends and family. Word of mouth spread, and soon I had a steady stream of clients. It wasn't a fortune, but it was enough to provide some financial relief.

Investing in my education and skills was another key strategy to grow my skills and in that, also increase my income. I took online courses to improve my photography skills and learned about digital marketing to promote my business better. Education empowered me to enhance my services and attract more clients, which in turn increased my income. When you start searching, you can also find free resources, instead of paying for training you do not have the budget for. But searching and going through trial and error can be more time-consuming, and yet still produce results in the end.

I opened my first studio in 2018 on a month-to-month contract, filled with nervousness as I was unsure if my business would sustain a studio. But it just started thriving. This little 'not a real job' business carried me through the divorce and through 2020 when the COVID-19 lockdown first started. I've managed to keep a heavy boat afloat, and this boat got even heavier when I became the sole financial provider for my children just over a year ago. In this time, I've seen some of the best and worst months in business. But I've managed to always keep food on the tables, the lights on, and have stationery, school uniforms, school bags and the necessary clothing ready.

I've been told to get 'a real job' because being a full-time photographer is not perceived as a real job. It's seen by many as that thing bored housewives start doing when their children go to school. Over the past years, I've worked hard on my business – the typical phrase 'blood, sweat, and tears' comes to mind – compared to my previous corporate years working in project management.

There are times when life just really knocks you around, and I ask, what am I supposed to do? Is the universe trying to tell me something, and I'm just not getting it, or just not listening? I'm so focused on just surviving that I can not find a way out. As we go through these motions, we keep pushing through. I remember last year when there were a few bad months in business and this was after several months when maintenance payments stopped coming in. Winter season started and my children needed winter school uniforms. To buy my children's winter school uniform, I sold unwanted items out of my home and studio.

This can sound very disheartening, but the items I sold were also extra-weight items. I looked around the flat and studio and for the first time in a while noticed items that brought back a slightly bad feeling or memory, like a negative energy. Things that came with the divorce or things I bought at times I don't associate positive feelings or memories with any longer. Essentially, as much as I needed the money to buy my children winter clothes, it was also a revitalising cleaning process. And how light life felt after that. I know for some this might sound strange, but the world is one big ball of energy and items also hold energy. This is my personal spiritual beliefs. This clean-up process lifted unwanted energy and also provided winter school wear for my children. The flip side of the coin is a win-win situation.

In the 2020 COVID-19 year, like many others, I had to sit at home with no income. For me, it was three months before I was allowed to work again. In those three months, we never went hungry. There used to be food for three days to seven days, all the time. We were so grateful for the community support. It was a challenging time around the globe, and I often think back at that time saying to myself 'You survived the 2020 lockdown, you can survive anything!'. Humans are resilient. We adjust to circumstances. There are moments we think 'I cannot do this', but we just do. We are so able to make things work even when we think we cannot. But it can also be exhausting and tiring to deal with this type of stress over long periods. It does wear a person down.

It was also during the start of the 2020 COVID-19 lockdown when I was first told 'It is time to get a real job'. And I remember thinking, 'Ya, that is easy for you to say with a law degree living in Canada where you secured a job before lockdown. And having a supportive partner. But right now, in South Africa, people are panicked. Companies are closing, laying people off, and reducing salaries. Where would a photographer get *a real job* now?'. I felt so disgruntled.

There were times in the years to follow when we were going through a bad patch, and I did look at going back to the workforce. But I was not even called for one interview. Unfortunately, being out of the workforce for as long as I have been, my skills are outdated. Even trying to work on the virtual assistant platform, you need to start at the bottom and work your skill sets up. I will not be making the big bucks straight away. But perhaps this is a possible backup plan.

This brings me to another point. Being a single parent, it is crucial to have a safety net or a backup plan. Because there is only one provider in the house it makes the safety net options smaller – only one income coming in which is often not even enough to cover the basics, never mind creating a safety net. We have to be prepared for the unexpected, and this is a constant subconscious or conscious stress. One thing we learned from COVID-19 is that life can change drastically, in a blink of an eye.

As mentioned earlier in the book, a single mother must fill every role in the house: protector, healer, teacher, nurturer, and also the provider. Part of the provider's role is not just to provide for today but also to make sure there are backup plans. Having a strong savings fund is one of the first steps, but this can be challenging at times when you don't make it through the month or something unexpected happens. Like when one of your suppliers accidentally closes his yard gate on your car and it cuts a hole in your car door. Even though I have insurance, I still need to come up with the excess, which ironically turned out to be slightly more than the actual repair cost. Ugh! Like I do not have enough to deal with already!

Another thing to look at is to have a testament in place if something were to happen to me. This is not a nice thought to have but it is the reality of life that unexpected things can happen. Hopefully, they never will, but one needs to be prepared. This ties in hand in hand with disability and pension funds. Again, we hope to live long healthy lives, but there are no guarantees. I would also hate to become a burden on my children in my old age and I sure do hope I can manage on my own financially, while they live their own healthy lives.

In South Africa, another thing to consider which is vital, is medical aid such as an entry-level hospital plan or medical insurance. Unfortunately, our government entities in South Africa are not in great condition and the private sector is very costly. But so many families (single and dual) struggle to afford this basic need. I discuss the effects of basic needs in Maslow's Hierarchy chapter. The bottom line is that a single mom has to do all this financial planning for the now and the future on her own. It is a big load to carry!

It's also important to teach children about money. I involved my children in budgeting and explained the importance of saving and spending wisely. These lessons are crucial for their future and help them understand our financial situation without causing undue stress. They are also at an age now where I can teach them that if they look after their clothes and toys, they can sell their unwanted items or clothing which they have outgrown as second-hand, and in the process make a bit of money. And if they break the hockey stick I bought them, they need to buy their own with their pocket money. The same goes for missing school jerseys. The struggle with them to look after their school uniform is unreal!

In conclusion, talking about income is vital, especially for a single parent. It requires transparency, planning, and sometimes difficult conversations. But by budgeting, seeking additional income sources, saving money, investing in education, and teaching our children, we can manage our finances effectively and provide a stable future for our families.

Living on a Tight Budget

So, how do I make things work on a tight budget? Honestly, some days, I feel like I'm just closing my eyes and pretending the problems do not exist, pushing through the best I can. Making tuna mayo sandwiches for dinner can be surprisingly fun. The children do not need to know that our options tonight are limited. Especially when they are small, they seem so blissfully oblivious to the empty spaces in the fridge and food cupboards.

As long as there is peanut butter, bread, and a few small yoghurt tubs, they are happy. When things go well, I shop for specials. Even if I do not need two more bags of washing powder, I buy the specials because in a few weeks, the washing powder at home will be finished and then I need to pay the full price. Sometimes you will find odd things piled up in my cupboards. Right now, I have several tubs of butter in the fridge, only one loaf of bread, and half a tub of peanut butter. For the next few months, I do not have to worry about running out of butter and having to pay the full price. The other day there was a massive discount and they were not close to expiring, so I stocked up!

It is fascinating how creative we can get with something like leftover stew or chicken. Instead of throwing away leftovers or even the last bit of gravy, I freeze them, no matter how small the portion. They come in handy for a quick lunch or can be added to couscous, a wrap, a pita, or pasta. Or rice if you need to cut back on gluten.

Another great trick with leftovers is Sloppy Joe's. Just open a can of baked beans, add it to a pot, and mix in any leftovers - spaghetti, stew, or the last bits of roast chicken. Add some spice or sauce (if needed), and dish it up on a burger bun or toast. Oh, and Friday night vetkoek (fat cakes) are always a party in our kitchen, even if we only have them with jam. The children love playing with the dough, trying to make the smallest possible fat cake.

Pancakes or flapjacks are always fun and inexpensive treats over weekends. During the week there is not always time. Sometimes, we focus so much on what the kitchen cupboards are lacking that we miss the creative opportunities right in front of us.

I am not scared of second-hand stuff - whether it's clothes, furniture, or camera equipment. I often buy second-hand. Depending on the item, it's important to do some research, compare prices, between new and second-hand, and weigh the pros and cons. Second-hand is not dead. Most of the furniture in my home is second-hand, and I just love giving them a new look with a bit of sandpaper, paint, and varnish. Just like that, you have yourself something pretty new.

In South Africa, we also have a lot of great markets, and this industry has boomed a lot since the COVID-19 pandemic, with people increasingly drawn to open-air markets instead of malls. Vintage has made a comeback, and nearly every market has a vintage section. I have bought decent winter jackets for myself for as little as R50. To put this in perspective, R50 in 2024 can buy a loaf of bread and a two-litre milk. And I love my jackets! Pair them with the right outfit and I am comfortable and stylish in my own way.

I giggle here because, depending on which side of town you walk, some admire your jacket and others give you a blank stare, thinking, 'Is she wearing that?'. But I hope you get what I am trying to say. Everyone's sense of fashion is different, and second-hand is not outdated. You can make it fashionable, and still feel good, with no need to compete with the blond name-brand brigade (no offence to blonds, there was a time I too did the blond highlights). Do also not forget to go visit your local thrift shops, until you find one that stocks items more in line with your style.

My denim jacket, with its little lace and pearl details, is just exquisite and I love wearing it out. It is more modern than my brown jacket, but the best part is, I bought it second-hand for R150. Bargain! There was also a blouse I bought, for R40. It was a brand name, still in great condition, but I never checked the size and later realised it was about two sizes too big for me. I hand-stitched some pleats on the shoulders and added a few buttons on the front, and it looked astounding. When I wore this blouse, people noticed and complimented me on how great my outfit looked with whatever pants or leggings I paired it with. I smiled, knowing how little it cost. I have never really been into brand names, but I do not mind wearing second-hand.

When my children were small and went to creche, I also bought them second-hand clothes because they would get so dirty at creche. There was no point in sending them to creche with new clothes. If I can find decent jackets and jeans for my children, I buy them. At the end of last year, I even bought my children second-hand school sports clothes as there was no budget for new ones. They're perfectly fine and happy wearing them to school. Among the other children, they all look the same.

I remember in 2020 during the COVID-19 lockdown, shopping with my children. There was no option to leave them home with another parent (cause there is only one – me), so off the three of us went, and I loaded them in the shopping trolley. As children are when you are in a shop, considering their ages and how oblivious they were to the struggles the world was facing at the time. Typical of children, they would ask for every second thing they saw. As a parent, you quickly learn the floor layout of the store and which aisles to avoid (aka, the toy aisles). But the stores know how we as parents think and will deliberately put things for children on the side aisles and by the checkout.

As a parent, we get fed up saying 'no' to all the 'I-want' questions or demands. And you cannot always just ignore them, because children start talking louder and louder, thinking mom did not hear, meantime mom is desperately trying to ignore them but cannot get away quickly enough as there is now a flipping trolley jam in the aisle and no way out...the frustration! But in these instances of 'I-want', I would simply answer them, 'I will buy that for you when I win the lotto' (in South Africa it is short for Lottery). And for some reason, that worked for quite a while to quiet them. The other people around would look at me strangely at first and then start laughing.

But soon my daughter got clever. Now she does not ask for things anymore, she hints straight out! She will pick something up or point to it and say something like 'Oh, look how pretty that is' (and describe the item in detail).

Or 'This looks so nice, I wonder what it tastes like'. I have forgotten the Lotto answer. Maybe I should start using that again. The best solution though is to try to do the shopping when they are at school. My new saving grace is online shopping, I am not sure why it took me so long to convert to online. It is bliss and also a heck of a lot easier to manage the budget by simply removing an item from your cart. There is no need to motor down iles again to check the price or to put it back. Another great thing which came about due to COVID-19.

There are currently two apps on my phone where I can shop at different shops and have my things delivered in an hour! Either way, doing the shopping when they are at school or online comes with a little more peace and quiet. I still often think, 'Do not worry, baby. When I win the lotto, I will buy you whatever you want.' As much as we can laugh and joke about winning the lottery, the reality is that one of the biggest burdens for many single mothers is finances. The other is unfair stigmas and stereotypes.

Financial stress is one of the biggest burdens on a large section of single moms. Due to this constraint, many single mothers have had to move back home with their parents. Some women do receive child maintenance, which is often not enough to cover the basic needs of their children. And many other women do not receive any child maintenance. This seems to be a global dilemma. Several of the studies I have read up on were conducted in different countries, and in each study, the results of the studies are roughly the same: the struggle to provide the basic needs for their children, such as food.

Financial burdens cause a lot of stress on households, leading to deep emotional and psychological stress and feelings of hopelessness, helplessness, and loneliness. Imagine it. Having a nearly empty food cupboard, not knowing what you will feed your children tomorrow. One mother explained that she would cut her food portions or skip meals, in order for her child to have a meal. How many people have been in this place before? How many people truly understand what hunger means?

In the UK, a study done by Stack and Meredith (2018) showed that one out of four children lived with a single parent and of these single parents, 86% are women of an average age of 38. They described feeling a bleakness to their circumstance and how the stress affected their health. They are constantly faced with problems such as the need for school uniforms for their children and social isolation as they cannot afford outings over weekends. These women feel embarrassed that they cannot afford a decent lifestyle for their children. Several of these women also struggle with exhaustion due to having more than one job.

This reminds me of the start of the COVID-19 lockdown when we saw the best and worst of humanity. Some people shared what they had, while others hoarded whatever they could find, even if it was through corrupt methods.

Financial Abuse

Financial abuse is a pervasive form of power imbalance found in various types of relationships, including marriages or partnerships. It often involves one person controlling access to money or concealing financial resources to keep the other person trapped in the relationship. This type of abuse can manifest in different ways, such as limiting access to bank accounts, monitoring spending, or preventing the victim from working or accessing education.

According to NNEDV.ORG, financial abuse occurs in 99% of domestic violence cases, highlighting its prevalence and damaging effects on individuals and families. This form of abuse can have long-lasting consequences, leading to financial instability, dependency, and difficulty in breaking free from abusive situations. Financial abuse is not just about money; it is a form of control that has deep emotional impacts on the victim. It is often linked with other forms of abuse, such as physical and sexual abuse, both during and after the relationship.

> 'Withholding funds for the victim or children to obtain basic needs such as food and medicine.' - National Network To End Domestic Violence.

> 'Withholding financial support like child support payments' – Wire

> 'Although it can happen to anyone, like other forms of family violence, the vast majority of violence is perpetrated by men against women.' – Wire

For single mothers, financial abuse can be particularly detrimental. It can take the form of withholding child maintenance payments, which are crucial for supporting the children. This tactic not only puts financial strain on the mother but also creates a sense of powerlessness and dependency. Additionally, abusers may use this tactic to manipulate the mother, spreading false narratives about her ability to provide for the children or using custody of the children as a bargaining chip. Some women have had to deal with the challenge of a defaulter who repeatedly failed to meet his financial obligations, leading to mothers and children being evicted and harassed.

It is important to recognise the signs of financial abuse and seek help if you or someone you know is experiencing this type of abuse. Support services and resources are available to assist victims in breaking free from abusive situations and reclaiming their financial independence, depending on the country you reside in. In South Africa, support is severely lacking.

Here is a first-hand personal story of a case of financial abuse to a woman and how she became the sole provider for her children. Their father immigrated with his new family to another country, with which South Africa does not hold a reciprocal order, ceasing all financial contributions the moment he left. Even in the month before his departure, there was no medical aid for the children, as he cancelled it early.

> 'The Reciprocal Enforcement of Maintenance Orders Act 80 of 1963 regulates foreign maintenance processes. It is a piece of legislation that makes provisions for South African parents to

> have their maintenance orders enforced in proclaimed foreign countries and vice versa.' – Burnett Attorneys and Notaries Inc.

Approximately a month before he departed from South Africa, he informed her of his plans through a brief message, stating that he resigned from his job and planning to leave the country the following month. Despite his departure, he provided no address, leaving discussions about maintenance and access agreements unaddressed. She still has no physical address for him, only a phone number and Gmail address which she was instructed to use for communication, despite requesting his physical address several times.

Her efforts to address maintenance issues were met with frustration, as her ex-husband played games by seeking a reduction in maintenance while simultaneously discussing the benefits of the new country for their children. Despite his promises to start the mediation process to discuss the changes which need to be made to the court order, he failed to follow through on his commitments, leaving her to question his true intentions. Two days before he left South Africa, he approached the local Family Court to request a reduction in maintenance. Knowing full well he will not be in the country for the court date a month later. The mother later attempted the mediation process as it can be done via zoom calls (no need for the father to be in the country, as would be required by the Family Court). Even during the mediation attempt, he would not commit to dates and times to start the session, claiming he could not afford it.

Nearly two years have passed since the added pressure began. Despite facing numerous challenges, including budget cuts, lack of medical aid, and the discontinuation of aftercare services, she ensures that her children have their basic needs met and clothes to wear to school, a luxury many other families in South Africa struggle to afford.

She grappled with the idea of allowing her children to move to the new country to live with their father, weighing the potential benefits against the uncertainty of their well-being in his care. His inconsistent behaviour, both before and after his departure, raised doubts about his ability to provide a stable environment for their children.

Even before immigrating from South Africa, he proved inconsistent in visitations and often made empty promises to their children. He showed sporadic and inconsistent behaviour, including periods of lavish gifts and outings followed by extended periods of neglect. Even though he lived less than 10 kilometres from them, he would go through an inconsistent period of six to eight months making no effort to see them. The only contact was via video call. And let me state again, he lived less than 10km from them. Then suddenly for a few months, there would be consistency which included the lavish spoils. It is for this reason that she could not consider moving her children to another country.

While acknowledging the potential benefits of the new country, including free schooling and medical aid, she remains steadfast in her belief that her children deserve more than being raised by a father who exhibits financial abuse. She believes it is not the government's responsibility to provide for her children's upbringing in place of their father's obligations. And that their best interests were not served by being used as pawns in a financial abuse game. She viewed his actions as a form of financial abuse, emphasising the importance of protecting her children from further harm.

How many other stories like these are there?

The National Network to End Domestic Violence hits the nail on the head with:
> *'Financial abuse is a common tactic used by abusers to gain power and control in a relationship.'*

Financial abuse is an insidious form of control that can begin subtly and escalate over time. Often disguised as care or concern, abusers may initially offer to take over financial responsibilities, promising to provide the victim with a weekly allowance. However, this seemingly generous offer can quickly turn into a means of control, as the abuser gradually reduces the allowance and takes full control of the finances. By the time the victim realises the extent of the abuse, they may find themselves without access to any funds or knowledge of the family's financial situation.

In more overt cases, financial abuse can involve threats of violence or intimidation to prevent the victim from working or accessing funds. This can leave the victim completely dependent on the abuser for financial support, further entrenching the power dynamic in the relationship.

Some common forms of financial abuse include deliberately draining resources during divorce proceedings and withholding child maintenance payments. Defaulters often use various tactics to delay legal processes, such as changing court dates or claiming ill health, leading to additional costs for the victim in seeking legal representation.

As I mentioned in my introduction as to what brought me to write this book, I stated that society seems to be well aware that so many (around 88%) of divorced fathers do not pay child maintenance. But do they get discriminated against? Okay, it could be easy for them to lie and say they are paying when they are not. Sadly, single mothers struggle financially and thus struggle to find rent places. Yet, the fathers continue their lives, and easily find places to rent, as if nothing is wrong.

I do think there should be a speedier process to prosecute them. It is a tedious process going to Family Court, which can take months, and without any guarantees, that the process will be implemented correctly. Many women have complained about how they feel the Family Court staff discriminate against them. The South African Maintenance Act is well laid down on paper but severely lacking implementation. Perhaps the previous suggestion to appoint the South African Revenue Services (SARS) to collect child maintenance, could be the magical answer.

Or perhaps it is just wishful thinking on my part…

As much as South Africa's legal system looks promising on paper, it is deeply flawed in the implication process, especially if a person can not afford an Attorney and is thus forced to work through the Family Court. If your case is not simple, you can count yourself lucky to get the needed help.

The Rules and Expectations

As a single mom, establishing rules and setting expectations is crucial for maintaining order and harmony in the household. It provides structure and helps my children understand what is expected of them, which is essential for their development and well-being.

I've laid down some quirky rules at home. You know by now I can swear or curse at times, and my children know that too. But we also have some fun, silly rules like:

No Coke, Pepsi, or coffee before they turn 10 (although they've had a sip here and there, not often, but they've been exposed).
No dating before sixteen (this rule might change, let's see how things go for now. They can casually date – whatever that means – and get more serious from sixteen. I'm figuring the rules out as we go).
They're only allowed to swear or use curse words after turning eighteen, as these are adult words. (It's working for now, but I doubt this rule will last until eighteen. Again, let's see how it goes).

Thus far, the rules seem to be working okay. Abby particularly finds them enlightening. Dean, on the other hand, respects the rules but also goes through phases of seriously testing boundaries and, in the process, my patience. I am flexible on the rules as we need to adjust as and when required. For their tenth birthday, we're planning a coffee date when they can enjoy their first coffee. They're excited, but I don't think they'll quite enjoy the taste of coffee unless it is loaded with sugar. I think sugar is far more dangerous and addictive than coffee.

That's a whole different discussion for a different time. And like most children, my children do love the sugary treats!

I teach my children to respect themselves, each other, and everyone they interact with. This means using polite language (cursing is for adults), listening when someone else is speaking, and treating others the way they would like to be treated. Respect is the foundation upon which all other rules are built. Homework comes next. Education is a priority in our home, and completing homework is a daily expectation. I encourage my children to tackle their assignments as soon as they get home from school. This habit helps them stay on top of their work and reinforces the importance of education.

In addition to these daily rules, I also set expectations for behaviour outside the home. Whether at school, at a friend's house, or in public, I expect my children to uphold the same standards of respect, responsibility, and kindness. These expectations help them navigate the world with confidence and integrity. Of course, flexibility is key. Life is unpredictable, and sometimes rules need to be adjusted. I believe in open communication and involving my children in discussions about our household rules. This approach helps them feel heard and valued, and it teaches them the importance of compromise and adaptability. And these are most days, not every day. Some days I just demand they get ready on time or we do not go out at all. In the perfect world, the perfect structure works. If you are perfect, raise your hand.

Screen time is something I regulate carefully. While technology can be educational and entertaining, it's essential to balance it with other activities. I set limits on how much time they can spend on their devices, ensuring they have plenty of opportunities for physical activity, reading, and family time. And yet, there are moments when the phone becomes a convenient 'baby sitter' keeping them busy while I work.

Chores are another essential part of our daily routine. Each child has specific tasks they are responsible for, such as making their beds, tidying up their rooms, and helping with the dishes. These chores teach them responsibility and the value of contributing to the household. It also lightens my load, allowing me to focus on other aspects of our lives. Abby however does not mind playing in the mud. But she thinks doing the dishes is gross. Getting her to do the dishes can sometimes be a battle.

They have to clean their rooms, every week, sweeping and mopping, and keeping them tidy the rest of the week. We have a tuck chart in the kitchen on the fridge. For each weekday their rooms are tidy, and they receive points. On weekends they get extra points for helping to cut the lawn and other tasks around the house. All this adds up to how much tuck money they receive on a Friday, to spend at the school tuck shop.

But there are also times I ask them to help around the house to make it a more cohesive place to live and bring harmony into the house. Tasks like packing dishes away, unpacking their school bags, emptying their lunch boxes before putting them in the sink, and opening the garage door and gates when we come and go. I do try my best to explain to them the concept of teamwork as we all live together and need to make it a functional and pleasant home for us all.

Society can also impose unspoken rules or expectations on a single mother. She should be financially independent and not needy. It's like there's a stereotype that single moms walk around with an empty tin begging for handouts. Like we have no dignity and drive to make things work? Yes, things get tough, but we don't want to stand on street corners begging. We do have dignity we'ed like to hold on to.

It's a single mother's role to find a way to provide for her children and herself. And yes, we know it. But sometimes people take for granted the strain on a single-income household compared to a dual-income household. It is for this reason I often hide how things are going, to avoid the judgment and presumption that I am hinting for the person to give me something. Something other than a hug. Often all a single mother needs is a simple, supportive hug.

Let's take a deeper dive. This isn't a case of two parents with one income, where both parents put their hands into the household and raising children. We're looking at a single parent with a single income trying to match up to society's expectation of financial independence as if she were part of a dual-parent household with dual incomes. This means the mother is working a full day, picking the children up, cooking dinner, helping with homework, getting her children off to bath and bed, cleaning up, and prepping for tomorrow, just to start the cycle over again the next day. Often single moms can not afford to get a domestic in to help. This means, the mother is here busy cleaning floors, doing the laundry and ironing at night. And yes, we get our children to help out with the tasks. It's a lot to manage on our own!

Then there's the issue of parenting standards or perceived lack thereof. When a single parent's children misbehave in public, it's a much bigger deal and frowned upon than when a mom and dad are together handling a meltdown. When a mom and dad are dealing with a public meltdown, the general response is, 'Ag, shame. Let's not stare and give them space to deal with their child.' If it's a perceived single mom, she gets death stares and judgment of how badly her children are behaving and can she not get them under control? I've received countless death stares in public. At times it felt like people were trying to stone me, or stab me with knives, with their eyes! Children have meltdowns. Gosh. It's not a single-mom thing, it's a child thing! I've had moments where I confronted people about rolling their eyes or asking if they've never seen a child throw a tantrum. But over time, I learned it's best to just ignore them as if they do not exist.

We're also expected to keep it together, meaning we need to have a good work and home life balance. And somewhere in between, we're allowed out to have a social life. But don't be too flashy with your social life, because who is now paying for that? Well, I had a really good month in business (my photography business, nothing inappropriate), after working my butt off. I decided to take my children out for a decent lunch or dinner at a nice restaurant. I worked for it and I am paying my own bills. Am I not allowed to enjoy the fruits of my labour?

Oh gosh, and this brings me to a completely different point that's not quite related to this chapter, or perhaps it is. There was a time when people thought I would do photography favours for them – shoots for free or at massive discounts. Just jaw-dropping. And don't get me wrong. I have often done photoshoots for free when people went out of their way to help me out, and I couldn't financially repay them. Even in cases when I needed to do a model call for a concept, I would first turn to my contacts list before asking on my social media pages to reach out to followers. These are not the instances I'm referring to. And not all my friends or associates have asked for favours.

Many have come to me as any other client, not expecting any favours in return and paying the normal price without any issues. They treated me and my business with respect, and for that, I am grateful. But there were a few with long stories wanting to constantly modify the package to try to get maximum results for minimal payment. Really? Or, they invite your children to the party in the hopes you take photos for free. And then give the subtle hint that they are paying for your child's meal and will even pay for yours. I'm not making this up! You are hustling the single mom who has to double up on everything she does! I quickly had to learn to say the big word...No. Just a No. It is a full sentence after all. No!

A single mom pretty much has to double up on everything she does for her family. Finding a balance between work, caring for her children, running the house, and caring for herself. It's a big hustle. When I am super focused on work to bring the money in, I tend to lack at running the house. When I am super focused on my children to give them as much possible attention, help with homework, help clean their rooms, and do all the sports run trips, I tend to slip up on business or social life. Doing a two-person job is still a two-person job, even when it is done by one person.

They say it takes a village to raise a child. But for some reason, it is difficult for a single mother to build this village. And I do think culture and family life play a big role in this. I have seen many clients from different cultures who have a strong village around them. But I have also seen mothers who struggle to build this village. Especially when they receive a lot of judgment and little support from their families, and often this is due to religious or cultural beliefs.

Who do you list as your emergency contact on school applications?

In some cultural groups, it would appear that single mothers are an embarrassment to that society. They would rather speak about them than to them.

Society's View

Sitting at the school dance the other night, one of the other mothers came over looking for her child, who is friends with mine. In the conversation, she explained that she, her husband, and her children needed to leave and wondered if I had seen her child. I explained I hadn't seen the group of friends but assured her I would tell her child she was looking for him when I did see them.

As she walked away, I couldn't help but ponder her dominant body posture. You know the one—where you make yourself bigger with your hands on your hips, arms pushed out, legs apart, and then lean forward, as if trying to tower over the other person. Coupled with the subtle display of contempt in her facial features and the slight increase in the pitch of her voice when she spoke about 'her husband,' it left an impression. Initially, I brushed it off, but it has me thinking about how I've experienced people talking down to me, especially after becoming a single mom.

Do married mothers feel superior to single mothers? It's not just women; men exhibit this behaviour too. On another occasion, my children and I went for a walk in our neighbourhood park and met some new neighbours. The woman and I had a lengthy conversation while her husband looked at me with a look of utter disgust. I was quite taken aback, as we had just met and I don't think we had even exchanged names yet. Honestly, I am not sure what that was about.

A friend pointed out that perhaps his stance was not related to me personally. Maybe he and his wife argued just before, and I mistook his demeanour as judgemental, as I've gotten so used to this kind of treatment. Who knows, perhaps I did make the wrong assumption that day.

This incident reminded me of some of the birthday parties my children have been invited to. Some of my daughter's school friends had birthday parties, and on the invite, the parents asked to stipulate if the parents were dropping their children off or staying at the restaurant. If you stayed, a large adult table was prepared, and your bill was for your account. This is quite normal around here. At two separate parties, I indicated that I would join.

At the first party, I was told to sit at the children's table with a brush of the hand, as there was no space left at the adult table. I am not kidding! Awkwardly, I went to sit at the children's table alone until I could find a waiter to seat me at a separate table nearby to still keep an eye on my children.

Months later at a second party, it happened again. The mother told me there was no space for me at their adult table, and the dad awkwardly tried to get a waiter to help me find a separate table. This time I was studying part-time and came prepared with my laptop and study materials, sadly expecting this kind of treatment.

Writing this down, it feels so strange, like it cannot be real that society would treat a person so bluntly like this.

On the second occasion mentioned earlier, I sat with my back to the long table where all the other parents and their children with siblings had great conversations. But I was not welcome to sit at the same table. Sadly, it was not the last time. By the next party, I arranged to do drop off. When someone wanted to invite me to sit down, I was quickly ushered away with, 'We will take good care of your children, you are welcome to go.' Maybe there are reasonable explanations for this. I don't know. But from the research done thus far, it seems to be the norm. Not just in South Africa, but pretty much globally!

I never realised there is a deadly disease called the 'Single Mother'. God forbid anyone catches it. On the contrary, the stereotypes and stigmas around single mothers are the actual diseases in society. I am not sure where the stereotypes and stigmas originated, but I do think religion played a big part when it demonised divorce due to the woman's lack of submission to her husband (irrespective of the actual cause for divorce, and there can be many valid reasons for divorce).

In the past, women were often blamed for divorce – she failed in her wifely duties or some other bizarre excuse for not being a good enough wife to her husband. It was almost as if a woman was expected to become a mother figure to her husband. Fortunately, today, this seems to be changing, and people are more open to understanding that there are many different reasons for divorce, and blame can be assigned to both sides.

It brings me back to the point that it takes a village to raise a child. Children need strong and stable societies to grow up in, and these societies extend outside the home. We also need to consider how societal stigmas affect the children, who are innocent in all of this, but nobody seems to take note of how it affects them.

I have covered a lot of the negative aspects, and society has a staggering focus on the negative aspects of the single mother, not even considering the enormous strength single mothers have for facing these difficulties. Not all single mothers live in dysfunction and poverty. Their circumstances are just disproportionate. Remember earlier when I mentioned a single mom with a single income, who gets compared with a dual-parent household and dual income, and how she expected to live up to the same standards? Not fair game, now, is it?

Single moms? They're the superheroes of the parenting world. Not only do they juggle the usual parental responsibilities, but they also seem to have a secret superpower: an increase in maturity and resilience. It's like single moms have cracked the code to be both; responsible and independent, all while raising their children to lead their own lives one day.

Single mothers are aware that they are not just raising children; they're raising future world-changers. Today's children – all the children - are the future. And the best part for single moms? They do it all with a sense of empowerment and liberation that is nothing short of inspiring. The single mother is stronger and more capable than how society has depicted her. Perhaps it was because of this pressure that she had to become strong and rise above.

For the most part, single mothers are involved in their children's lives, which creates stronger relationships and bonds. Even though I am shining single mothers up in this beautiful trophy cabinet, as strong as we are, we don't always feel it. We don't always have our shit together. But we do our best.

The narrative surrounding single mothers is overwhelmingly focused on the negative outcomes rather than their numerous strengths constructed in the face of difficulty. Many of the positive attributes of this group, such as resilience, maturity, and egalitarian gender role beliefs, are often pathologised and painted as risk factors. For example, one study found that teachers were more likely to consider a child of a single parent to be a liar, unintelligent, and bad (Torres-Mackie, 2020).

Stigma can be divided into three categories: morality, sex role violations, and victimisation. These negative perceptions towards single mothers pose significant obstacles for them to play their role effectively within society.

As encouraging as this can be and true for many, many other single moms struggle to keep the lights on and face daily challenges. A lot of single moms do not have any financial support. Many single mothers receive little to no financial support from their children's fathers because they use financial abuse as a weapon against the mothers, as previously discussed. A single mom can choose to buckle under it or rise above it.

The Single-Mom's Burden on Society

There's a lot of stereotyping around single mothers, even in the dating scene. I was once told to wait until I was fifty to start dating. The woman who told me this rambled about how people find love in their fifties and still have great sex lives. Keep in mind, that she is still married to her first husband. What I am trying to say is she has not experienced divorce personally. It made me wonder, am I not allowed to find love and happiness while raising children ? Am I not worthy while my children are still at home? Or am I just a parasite on society? Are married women scared of single mothers, fearing they'll steal their husbands or have an affair? Are single moms seen as villains who seduce married men? How much truth is there behind these ideas, and how much is just stereotype? These questions linger, as statistics on affairs are hard to measure, with many going unreported. More on affairs will be discussed later.

Affairs are just one aspect of the stigma around single mothers. In many studies I found, from different countries, similar issues were highlighted, such as:
Being blamed for the divorce and labelled as having a setback in life.
Assumptions that they gave birth at a young age.
Being perceived as having poor mothering skills.
Association with poverty.
Being seen as living immoral lives due to lacking the proper morals to succeed in society.
Being thought to suffer from psychological illness or substance abuse.

In an online study into the difficulties single mothers face, stigmatisation emerged as a heavy burden. Single mothers can be classified as either good or bad. A woman might be seen as a good single mother if she became a widow, but if she became single through divorce, she is often judged as a bad mother (Rusyda et al., 2011). Numerous studies highlight how single mothers are judged and repeatedly not seen as worthy or fully part of society due to their 'single' status. This raises the question: does this judgment play into the sympathy society feels obligated to give single mothers? In a study by Karunanayake et al. (2021), single mothers reported that society sympathises with them, but often in a negative manner. As a result, many single mothers avoid appearing weak and instead put up a facade of strength. This phenomenon is summarised by the following quotes from study participants:

'When a single mother goes out of the house, the whole crowd looks at her.' (Participant C1)
'I think there is a huge difference in how society treats a mother and a single mother.' (Participant C3)
'I think time should teach others about what we are going through in our lives. Because I cannot put astray my children for the sake of being a single mother. I have to fulfil their duties alone in society.' (Participant A1)

In some studies, the stigma was so severe that some women were not even permitted by their neighbours to participate in rituals during events of any religious nature. Is this due to the perceived shame these women bring to society? That they are not worthy and no longer hold a valid space in society? Is this the reason why I was not allowed to sit at the same table with the other parents at the kiddies' birthday parties?

The shocking reality is that many married or partnered mothers never seem to think they might find themselves to be single mothers. And let's face it, who gets married to get divorced (Okay, there are probably some wackadoodles out there)? Yet, we get car insurance just in case something happens. Single mothers are often regarded as hindrances in society, with assumptions and gossip spreading about them. Several participants in the studies mentioned that their neighbours stopped talking to them but talked about them. Even those close to the single mothers gossip about them, including family members and old friends.

Many of the women in the studies reported how they held high status in society when they were married and had a stable income. After the divorce, they were deemed of lower value in society. Neighbours, friends, and family who used to welcome them with open arms now look down on them and discard them as unequal individuals of lower value.

These negative perceptions have become the norm for single mothers. I myself have experienced this with a friend whom I have known since school. At one stage after the divorce, I used to visit her family as often as possible but sadly realised that gossip was being spread behind my back. Since then, I have distanced myself from her and her family and have not visited since.

When a single mother actually does relatively well for herself, is that a bad thing? Does it evoke jealousy?

On another front, a lot of judgment is made about a single mother who tries to date. Men see them as coming with baggage (as if they don't have any themselves). Some of the things being said are: The divorce was probably her fault. She will fixate on her children, and the men do not have the time for that. And her body looks weird. Wait, what!? So, your wife who gave birth, her body is not weird? Does a woman's childbearing body change after a divorce compared to childbirth? Or are men just saying things they think about their wives/girlfriends, but do not dare to say? Now they project this onto the single mother? And of course, a single mother will be concerned for her children. SHE IS THE ONLY PARENT AFTER ALL - assuming baby daddy (South African slang for fathers) is no longer actively involved with his children. Meaning he does not see them anymore and does not financially contribute. Do the occasional phone calls count as being actively involved when the children have not seen their father in six months or longer, who lives 10 km away, other than on a video call?

Torres-Mackie (2020) did a beautiful dissertation on the stigmas of single mothers and their children. From this, I want to quote the explanation of stigma:

'Social stigma, or simply stigma, is defined as the devaluation of individuals and groups based on personal characteristics that are regarded as deviant, usually because they depart from dominant cultural norms. Stigma also pertains to the shame that an individual may feel as a result of such disapproval from others.'

An interesting point made in this dissertation is that other non-traditional families were not affected by the same stigmas as single mothers. Families such as single fathers, same-sex parents, spouses who choose not to have children, and interracial couples apparently do not suffer the same level of judgment and rejection from society.

If the single-mother family is also untraditional, what makes them such a disgrace in society? Why are they perceived as a 'threat' and deviant? The single mother has to continue functioning in an environment that judges and criticises her, affecting both her and her children. Yes, it affects her children as well. The irony is that society takes more empathetic sympathy for the single father and sees him as more capable of raising children alone. A study with 1351 participants indicated that they see single fathers as more competent than single mothers. This study is based purely on people's opinions and viewpoints, not a parent's ability to raise children – no facts, just opinion. He is seen as a good provider, competent, responsible, and leading a good life. The irony in this, for those father's who do not pay child maintenance!

Now, this makes me wonder. Are these assumptions made purely based on financial capability, considering men generally earn 30% more than women? Is money the only thing it takes to raise a child? And then we see how few divorced or separated fathers actually pay the maintenance. How flawed is humanity's perspective and bias?

If this were a game between the sexes, it would be an unfair game with different rules for different sides. Even today, it is reported women struggle to stand out in the corporate world. Only about 20% of managerial positions around the globe are held by women. Men are more likely to receive promotions and managerial positions than women, as men are seen as more capable of and best suited for managerial positions (Schein et al., 2001).

In the workforce, the excuse for women is often related to her attention being divided between her work and family life. So here, her family life is the excuse for the promotion, and in the role of a single mother, she is viewed as just plain incompetent. Is this perhaps a global female stereotype of a woman being the lesser and weaker human form?

Look at the study done by Gneezy (2006) which shows that competitive drive is not hereditary. Studies were done in two opposite civilisations. In one, men were raised to be more dominant and more competitive; in the other, women as childbearing were raised more dominant and competitive. It is quite interesting as it indicates the effect of how society raises children as either competitive or not. Thus, women are just as competent as men in the workforce and managerial positions.

Karunanayake et al. (2021) showed that children from single-mother homes fare nearly the same or better than children from single-father homes.

Women are capable of bringing life into this world. Her womb carries a child, and she gives birth to this child. She is capable of nurturing, caring, and raising her child. Women, all women! This includes the single mother as she too is a woman.

The Effect of Stigmas and Stereotypes on Children

These stereotypes and stigmas not only affect single mothers but also have indirect implications for their children. For several weeks, my two children have been trying to arrange playdates with some of their friends from school. Despite having the parents' numbers and attempting to make arrangements, the other parents have repeatedly postponed appointments or come up with excuses. One parent even told her son that she messaged me and I did not reply, blaming me when I never received the message. How do I explain to my children that society does not accept me as a single mother, thus the reason for all the excuses for a playdate? Do my children really deserve this treatment? They did not choose these circumstances; they came into this world with innocence.

In the US, studies have shown how children in single-parent homes have increased from 20% to 33% (Torres-Mackie, 2020). This study also revealed teacher-biased treatment towards children in single-parent homes. Children from single-parent homes are often regarded as having low intellect, being naughty, undisciplined, incompetent, and with low future prospects, all based on opinions and not facts.

Yet, the facts show the opposite. Children from single-parent homes are often more competent, ambitious, motivated to succeed, resilient, self-sufficient, and generally have higher self-esteem. They understand their responsibilities in the household and their environment from a young age. Indirectly, they become aware of the views on single mothers, building resilience and a drive to rise above these perceptions, as they are surrounded by these attitudes in society. They have faced more challenges than most children from a younger age.

> *Amelia shared,*
> *'When growing up, I'm like, my Mom is both. I was like, well, my Mom is my Mom and my father, but I was like, she's a woman and a man. She can do anything, in my eyes, when I was growing up. Cooking, cleaning, literally building anything, getting on her hands and knees and dirty; whatever kind of man role that there needed to be, she would do it, and I loved that.' (Torres-Mackie. 2020)*

Children from single-parent homes develop these beautiful qualities:

Internal Wellbeing:

> The fascinating world of children of single mothers and their unique abilities contribute to their personal satisfaction. Unlike seeking external validation, these capacities focus more on internal contentment. The key themes identified are Reflectiveness, Empowerment, and Freedom from Convention.

> Reflectiveness:
> > Children of single mothers tend to be quite introspective, likely due to their keen awareness of how others perceive them. This self-awareness helps them navigate their place in the world. Some participants even described it as being curious about

themselves and their surroundings, a trait that ultimately empowers them.

Empowerment:
Despite facing societal stereotypes, children of single mothers often feel a strong sense of empowerment. They come to realise their own strengths and develop strategies to tackle challenges head-on. This newfound confidence often stems from shouldering responsibilities early on and achieving their goals.

Freedom from Convention:
Growing up in non-traditional family structures, children of single mothers often embrace their uniqueness and defy societal norms. They prefer to chart their own course rather than adhere to conventional expectations. This independence allows them to pursue happiness on their own terms.

Overall, these qualities help children of single mothers build a strong sense of self-worth and appreciate their individuality, leading to a positive sense of well-being.

Adversity Management:

Children of single mothers learned how to navigate hardship. Raised in environments where it's often 'sink or swim', children of single mothers develop skills to manage adversity, setting them apart from peers who may not face similar challenges. Adaptability, Resourcefulness, Acceptance of Reality, and Self-Sufficiency are key themes in their approach to handling difficulties.

Adaptability:
>Children of single mothers learn to be flexible and tolerate change, adapting to manage challenging situations.

Resourcefulness:
>They develop problem-solving skills through inventive means, often due to early responsibilities and limited resources.

Acceptance of Reality:
>Children of single mothers acknowledge difficult situations and move forward, using challenges as opportunities for growth.

Self-Sufficiency:
>Growing up, children of single mothers learn independence and self-reliance, becoming adept at managing problems on their own.

These capacities, though often strengths, can also pose challenges if not balanced properly. Overall, children of single mothers' ability to manage adversity stems from their early experiences, shaping them into resilient individuals who tackle difficulties head-on.

Ability to Achieve:

Children of single mothers develop key capacities that shape their ability to succeed. These include Diligence, Perseverance, and Self-Efficacy, all of which are influenced by their early experiences as children of single mothers.

Diligence:
Children of single mothers often exhibit a strong work ethic, driven by a need to prove others wrong, witnessing their mothers' hard work, or managing responsibilities independently from a young age.

Perseverance:
This is about pushing through challenges to achieve goals, even without immediate rewards. Children of single mothers learn to tolerate discomfort and keep working towards their objectives.

Self-Efficacy:
Children of single mothers believe in their ability to achieve their goals. This belief stems from managing multiple responsibilities at home and successfully handling various challenges.

These capacities, developed in response to the challenges faced as children of single mothers, continue to influence their approach to achieving success in adulthood. They learn to work hard, persevere through difficulties, and believe in their ability to accomplish their goals, setting them apart as resilient individuals with a strong sense of self-worth.

Interpersonal Function:

Growing up as a child of a single mother influences individuals' empathy, social justice mindset, and maturity.

Empathy:
Many children of a single mother develop empathy through their experiences, such as witnessing their mothers' sacrifices or taking on responsibilities at a young age. This empathy extends to understanding others' struggles and perspectives.

Social Justice Mindset:
Feeling different from others, children of single mothers often develop a sense of social justice, recognising and advocating for marginalised groups. This mindset stems from their own experiences of feeling marginalised and connects them with diverse communities.

Maturity:
Due to early responsibilities, children of a single mother often mature faster than their peers. They become more capable of handling adult situations and

responsibilities, leading others to perceive them as mature beyond their years.

These interpersonal capacities shape how children of a single mother relate to others and navigate the world, highlighting the resilience and unique perspectives they develop from their upbringing.

Gender Roles:

Gender Role Agency is like having a VIP pass to the gender norms party, but instead of sticking to the usual script, you're free to rewrite your own lines. Participants in the study found themselves breaking free from conventional gender expectations, thanks to their upbringing as children of single mothers.

They were not just marching to the beat of society's gender drum; they were conducting their own symphony. From sharing household responsibilities regardless of gender to embracing a more fluid understanding of masculinity and femininity, these folks were rewriting the gender rulebook one chapter at a time.

While some might raise an eyebrow at their gender-bending antics, these participants saw it as a badge of honour. They were not just challenging gender norms; they were flipping them on their head and giving them a good shake.

For them, gender self-efficacy was not just a buzzword; it was a way of life. They did not need a permission slip from society to be who they wanted to be. They were the architects of their own gender destiny, building a future where gender stereotypes were nothing more than relics of the past.

I do hope that some of the people reading this book who were raised by a single parent can relate and see these qualities within themselves. And perhaps the current generation of single-mother children will change the dynamics of society's view on single mothers.

Children are the future, whether a single parent raises them or not. They may play a small role in society now, but later, they will rule it. Your children and my children are our future society. We cannot pretend your problems are not mine, and vice versa, and that we can operate separately. Our children will have to navigate this society together in just a few short years.

The Maslow Hierarchy

Earlier, I discussed the challenge of juggling a full-time job, managing children's school work, and running the household. Now, let's add part-time studies to the mix. Where does a mother find the time for all this? You give up a few more hours of sleep. Ideally, we should get around eight hours of sleep a night. But you'd be surprised how the body can adapt to less for a while, until there's a crash, and then the cycle starts all over again.

You've probably heard about Maslow's hierarchy of needs for motivation. It's this triangle that explains the different levels a person needs to fulfil in their lives to move on to the next level, ultimately reaching self-actualisation. Self-actualisation refers to a person reaching self-fulfilment in their potential, being themselves, and living their full potential. Many of us are still trying to figure out our potential and might be a bit stuck on some of these levels, not yet reaching the fifth one. For single mothers, we are often stuck between the first and second levels.

From the moment we wake up, our day is filled with thoughts, often fearful thoughts. 'What are we making for dinner today? Is there enough food to pack the lunch boxes? Is there enough fuel in the car for the week's school run? Seasons are changing soon. What clothes still fit my children and how many new clothes do they need?' With these worries hanging over our heads all day, it's difficult to reach the third level, reaching love and relationships with others and often with our children. Our tempers are short as we are constantly worried about the lack, not having enough, worrying about what my children would need for today and tomorrow. These stresses can cause me to be distracted. I struggle to pay attention to their stories of the day, and the chit-chat in the car. The stress and worry about tomorrow become all-consuming, making it difficult to live in the moment. Single mothers tend to be on high alert most of the time.

Here is an abstract of Maslow's writings explaining the dynamics of a hungry man, and what his world looks like:
> 'Another peculiar characteristic of the human organism when it is dominated by a certain need is that the whole philosophy of the future tends also to change. For our chronically and extremely hungry man, Utopia can be defined very simply as a place where there is plenty of food. He tends to think that, if only he is guaranteed food for the rest of his life, he will be perfectly happy and will never want anything more. Life itself tends to be defined in terms of eating. Anything else will be defined as unimportant. Freedom, love, community feeling, respect, philosophy, may all be waved aside as fripperies which are useless since they fail to fill the stomach. Such a man may fairly be said to live by bread alone.' (A Theory of Human Motivation by A.H Maslow, 1943. Originally Published in Psychological review, 50, 370-396. https://psychclassics.yorku.ca/Maslow/motivation.htm)

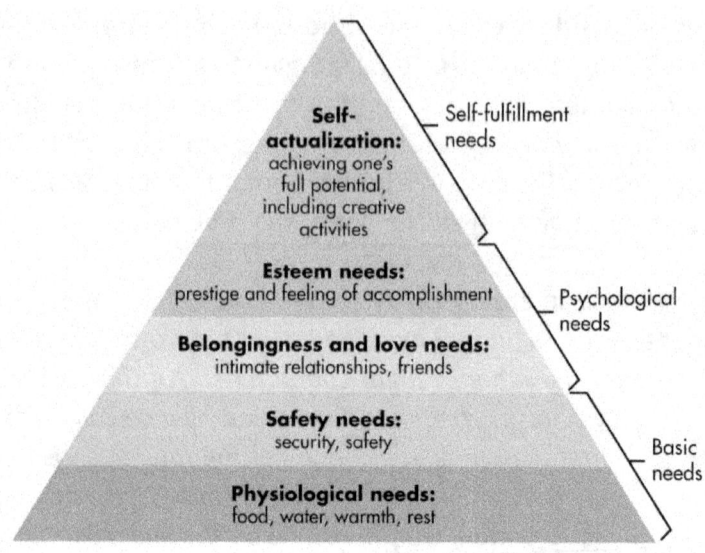

https://www.simplypsychology.org/maslow.html

Initially, the thought about this hierarchy is that a person needs to fulfil the first level before they can successfully move on to the second level. When a person is hungry, all they can think of is food. They cannot think about personal development or contributing to their community. However, putting this into practice, it has been found that it is possible to have parts of one layer of needs met to find some fulfilment on a higher level.

It is possible for a person dealing with financial constraints to feel loved and supported by the people closest to them. For a single mother living with family, she has emotional support and acceptance, even though society has discarded her, and she still deals with the daily financial constraints to provide for her children.

The first level is where the single mother is focused on being able to provide food and shelter for her children. We have looked at this quite a bit already in the budget chapter. Every human being needs food and water, a safe place to sleep, and appropriate clothes to wear.

The second level is safety needs. Here the single mother focuses on providing a safe home environment, a stable income, protection for her and her children, and possibly healthcare (which we know in South Africa, decent medical aid is quite costly).

The third level is belonging and love needs. Here a single mother will look for social connections and support (try to build a village for her and her children). A community in which they feel loved and accepted.

The fourth level is esteem needs. Here it becomes more of a level of hope for recognition, respect, and self-esteem. For the effort they put into parenting, their community, and their work.

And then the fifth level is self-actualisation. The highest level is where one realises one's full potential and personal growth. Here the single mother might start pursuing further education, career, or personal development goals.

A lot of single mothers are faced with the challenges of basic needs, the first two levels. Having these levels mostly fulfilled does create a sense of achievement and feeling fulfilled and more positive about the outlooks of life. She also might receive plenty of support and acceptance from her home environment where family and close friends support and admire her courage. But the opposite happens in society, which then affects one's self-esteem.

The hard judgments from society can be very difficult and emotionally bear on any person.

According to Maslow's theory, as humans, we have a need to understand our environment and to make sense of the world. We need to learn new information as this helps us meet our other needs (Hopper, 2020).

At times, I have felt very overwhelmed with a loss of purpose. For the past couple of years, my focus has solely been to provide for my children and keep them safe. There have been times when I wondered who I am outside of my family responsibilities and felt that my work has lost all meaning other than a means to an end.

My passion and drive for creativity and photography have been smothered by the constant fear of failing to provide for my children , along with the need to stay ahead of bills and plan for the next big expense, such as stationary or winter clothes.

It can make managing these hierarchy levels very tricky when your life is so out of balance, constantly moving up and down between levels. One minute you are at the bottom, fighting to get the basics done, and the next minute you are in the middle, appreciating your friend for taking the children for a day so you can have a moment of silence in your life.

Another perspective is a single mother's perceived masculinity. Single mothers are engulfed with both father and mother responsibilities, which can be conflicting. In the midst of this, they deal with public opinion and criticism. There are a lot of masculine tasks a single mother needs to learn, not because she wants to be more masculine, but out of necessity. Due to this, she gets judged for being too masculine, and because of this egalitarian approach, she gets demonised.

I have my own toolbox and drill. It is not a perfect toolbox; it is quite messy but has most of the odds and ends I need from time to time. Just because I know how to drill a hole, put a lug and screw in, does not mean I enjoy doing these things. No, I don't. But I do not have a father or brother who can come around and help out with the handy work. Thus, I had to learn. If there was a man around the house to do these things, I would definitely be asking him to do this.

The same goes for the braai. I like the idea of teaching my son how to start a fire and how to braai. There is no father around to teach him this. And I come from a culture where a braai was very common over weekends. From a young age, I learned how to start a braai by spending time with family around the fire and observing. Then the day came when a female flatmate and I had a few friends over and we wanted to braai. We were all females, and fortunately, I knew how to start the fire.

The other day, a female friend and I took my children fishing. They were gifted fishing rods, which had been lying in the garage for some time. And there is no man around to teach them how to fish. So, my friend said she knows how. And off we went, making a picnic out of it. I am not going to lie; it was odd to see two women with two children next to the fishing waters. Some people did stare at us. Fortunately, two guys nearby helped us make the knots into the fishing lines and showed us how to get the casting right as we were under a tree standing next to the water. And the few times the lines got stuck in the trees, they helped us get it out. In the end, my children had fun sitting next to the fishing waters for a while.

We do these things out of necessity, not because we think we are better than men or in most cases think we don't need a man. A woman who says she does not need a man probably has had very traumatic experiences. Do not judge her without knowing her story.

As mentioned at the start of the book, never actually noticed the whole stigma of the single mother until my recent relocation experience. There were times I was not even allowed to view a property, with silly excuses that there was an application in progress (yet the property stayed available online for weeks after) or I was told I didn't earn enough, yet I had a good credit record and a letter from my accountant confirming my income as above the required minimum requirement, as stipulated in the adverts. Even trying to get my children into a new school came with a large amount of stress, and in the end, I turned to the Department of Education for assistance.

The amount of stress this move at the end of 2023 caused, and the tears I cried because it felt like everything possible was going wrong. On a Friday morning, I finally got approval for a property to rent. But I cannot move to the other side of the city if my children cannot get into a new school. After struggling that whole week already to get the school application even looked at and visiting the Department of Education's office, a midday call came through to tell me no, it is not happening this year. I just sat in my chair at work and sobbed and sobbed and sobbed, wondering how can it be this hard. All I am trying to do is get my children into a good school, move closer to the area where most of my clientele are based, and in the process make some budget cuts to try to improve our quality of life.

An hour later, the department phones and tells me my children need to be at the new school on Monday at 7 am in school uniform. Fuck, I jumped, and tears started flooding my face again with relief and joy. There was no time for my children to even say goodbye to friends. I literally had to rush to pick them up and drive all the way to the other side of the city to go buy school uniforms. And this after a quick call, still in tears, to the agent to say my miracle arrived and we can move into the house in the next week. That's right, things started falling in place at the last minute, or technically, right at month end. Four days to month end.

Those fucked up moments when life just knocks you around. Now, when I planned this move, it was supposed to take place during my study term break (which also happened to be over the school term break) so as to not interfere with my studies. But that was just not how life turned out. In the two weeks after we moved, I had my two final assignments due. I had to unpack every single box in 2 days to get my home set up and studio ready for my first photography client. With this, continued with the normal study load as well as completed my two final assignments to pass my study modules. The first assignment was done in a reasonable time. But by the second one, I was so exhausted, catching up on weekly study activities, juggling life, my children who were also busy with year-end assessments (they walked in on the start of assessments on their first Monday!) and dealing still with the chaos of finding our feet after the sudden move (which was in planning for months but had to happen in a few days). I was exhausted, not sure if I already mentioned it. But one more assignment and a week's study work to do.

My last assignment was done in 24 hours, with intense research, a 2000-word essay, and exhaustion. I ended up submitting it a bit late, which caused me to be penalised. But at least I passed it with a C. I am still not sure how I managed to pass my last term with all the chaos of the move, but I am relieved that I did pass.

At that point, I did not have to worry about something as basic as food, as business was going well. I did, however, start depleting savings due to the move, which slowly started building up stress again to have a good safety net available in case shit hits the fan.

Looking at Maslow's hierarchy, one can see how if the basic needs, the first two levels, are not strong, it can lead to a whole lot of stress and imbalance in a person's life.
A mother needs to protect her daughter from the dangers of the world, and she needs to have a strong, disciplined hand for her son who needs a male role model in his life. There is so much complexity in the life of a single mother, and on top of it all, the unfair judgment of society.

Single mothers face several challenges to meet their basic needs while striving for self-actualisation, as described by Maslow's hierarchy of needs. It highlights the daily struggles of providing food, shelter, and safety for their children, often leaving little room for personal growth and fulfilment. Single mothers encounter so many societal stigmas and judgments, which can further impact their self-esteem and emotional well-being. Through personal anecdotes and examples, the chapter underscores the resilience and adaptability of single mothers as they navigate these complexities.

Medical Emergencies

Oh, the funny stories. Not at all funny at the moment, but you do end up laughing about it later.

After our big move, end of last year, within the first three weeks, my son cut himself twice with glass on his hands. The first time was a small but slightly deep cut, which fortunately healed well without needing medical treatment. I could doctor it at home with the medical kit. The second time was more serious, and stitches were possibly required.

Fortunately, by this time, I had joined the neighbourhood WhatsApp group and could ask for advice on which hospital to go to. Being new in the area and still using GPS just to find the shops for bread and milk, I had no clue where the nearest hospital was.

To make matters worse, this happened after 7 pm, and we were all already in our pyjamas. To our amazement, one of our neighbours was a paramedic and he came to look. He managed to help us patch up the cut with the right plasters, so we did not need to rush to the hospital. We were very grateful for the help, considering we did not have medical aid and would either have to pay the private hospital cash or spend the night at a government hospital waiting for treatment.

For weeks after this, I was jumpy whenever something fell or sounded like something was breaking. So much so, that I did not even want my children to use normal glasses, but plastic cups for a month.

My daughter, Abby, split her chin open twice before she officially turned 10. The first time was a fall when she was around two-and-a-half years old while we were busy removing carpets to tile the floors. It was not a very deep cut, and the doctors could use glue instead of stitches.

The second time was shortly after her brother's finger-cutting incident. We were invited to a street braai to meet the neighbours. Off we went with a picnic basket and camp chair in hand, down the street. I told my children to ride their rollerblades because I wasn't sure if there would be other children to play with. Things are all social. Another child arrived on his bike, and my son went home to get his bike. A short moment later, Abby also wanted to ride her bike, but I said no, explaining that her bike's brakes did not work and it would be safer on the rollerblades... Little did I know how I would eat my words not long after when she came down the street, lost her balance, and bam, hit the tar!

For a moment, it looked like she froze. I ran to help her and get her out of the road. At first, I did not realise how bad her chin was. I called the paramedic neighbour again, apologising for needing his help, but he assured me it was okay. A few minutes later, he arrived, took a look at Abby's chin, and confirmed what I feared. This time, we needed to go to the hospital for stitches. Long story short, we are off to the hospital, a private hospital as a cash client. We still had no medical aid and had to pay for treatment upfront. Unfortunately, most government hospitals are of such poor standards, that you would risk bankruptcy at a private hospital rather.

Another problem, besides having to pay cash when I could barely cover the basic bills, was that Abby had made up her mind she did NOT want stitches! I casually discuss this with her in the car, trying to calm her fears. All went well upon arriving at the hospital. They checked her wounds and gave her a colour rating based on the severity of the injury (which was not a high rating), and she is still very calm and collected.

We were then taken to a treatment room, and everything was still going well. The second nurse went over everything and prepped for the doctor to start. Abby asked many questions, and we watched YouTube videos to see how oxygen flows through the bloodstream. Very fascinating cartoon animations, nothing gory or stressful. The doctor arrived, and everything was still going well. We explained the process to her, including the injection, which was exactly the same as what she had several times at the dentist. The doctor numbed the area on her chin, and even though she squealed a bit, it still went well. But when the doctor came close with the stitches needle that looked like a tiny hook, all hell broke loose. She just refused to have her stitches done!

Two hours later, we were still struggling with Abby to get her stitches in. I walked the corridor with her, showing her the hospital was not a scary place. We tried talking through her fear and doing breathing exercises, but nothing worked. They brought the first sedation, a little tube thing Abby needed to inhale. But she is resisting it and completely faking it. At one stage, she appeared to be passed out. Both the nurse and I were sure Abby was asleep. I tickled her feet and under her arms with a pen, but she remained still. The nurse was about to call the doctor, but I knew my child and stuck my finger in Abby's ear. She jerks up laughing. I am annoyed as shit! The nurse was first surprised, then despondent – completely understandable. It was time to step up the game.

Another nurse arrived shortly after with a different medication. By now, I had tried bribing Abby with extra tuck money, staying calm, swearing, and even threatening to leave. But nothing worked. She was adamant she did not want stitches, even though her chin still dripped blood every few minutes. The second medication was administered (with some effort), and we could all see it was making her drowsy.

Even then, half out of it, she still freaked out when the tiny hook needle appeared. It ended up taking four nurses to hold her arms, legs, and head still so the doctor could stitch her up. She is a feisty young girl, I must say. Even after the doctor was done with the four stitches (only four), she was still adamant she did not want them! Unfortunately, the wound was of such a nature that stitches were needed to help it heal without infection.

This was a very traumatic experience for all involved: Abby, the nurses, the doctor and me. Even the next day, I could feel the stress in my body. This experience can evoke many different opinions and feelings. If the nurses had not held Abby down, she would have needed to be admitted to the hospital, stay the night, and be administered anaesthesia. Which, the mother, AKA me, did not have the money to pay for.

The next step would have been to discharge her and we would have had to drive to a government hospital, for her to be admitted for anaesthesia. In a government hospital, we probably would have sat in an overcrowded emergency room for hours, waiting just to see a doctor. It was a difficult situation, and we did the best we could.

Abby was absolutely fine the next day. Her bruises from the fall (knees, one elbow, and her chin) were tender from the actual fall. The following day, she was back at school, laughing about the experience and showing off her stitches to her friends.

The moral of the story is to have medical aid or medical insurance at least in South Africa. The very next day I got us all on medical insurance. I am not yet sure how I am going to pay for it, but I will make a plan. Sole provider or not, we make a plan.

I must add a note here that the only Government hospital experiences I have encountered were with my late father. The conditions at the different hospitals he went to were not great, at all. And it is not the fault of the nurses and doctors, who have to work in such poor conditions – overcrowded hospitals, understaffed and lacking supplies.

Single, NOT Ready to Mingle

Returning to an earlier comment about the single mom supposedly wanting the married woman's husband, I was not trying to sound rude or anything like that. It is just tricky to steer through society as a single mom. There are so many challenges we face, and the stereotypes that we act promiscuously and are on the hunt. My motto is simple: if he cannot be faithful to you as his wife and mother to his children, he will not be faithful to me. For me, this is a no-brainer.

There are many broken relationships and marriages, and many people who do get involved with a married person. I do understand it from a woman's perspective. On the flip side, the single mom can sometimes be perceived as desperate for love and affection, making her easy to manipulate.

Men chase the single mom, testing the waters, flirting with their eyes, or even worse, telling you that they are separated. Only to hear two days later that they fixed things up and are living together again with their wives (technically, he never lived separately during this so-called separation). It is difficult for single women to navigate through all this bullshit! And that is what it is. Just bullshit. Do you know how easy it is for a woman to gain a bad reputation?

A little story: girl meets boy. The girl is already divorced and knows it is a long process of being separated before the divorce gets finalised. The boy makes small advances. First just little jokes, then coffee with 'business intentions', all creating mixed signals. Then the jokes and online chats become more frequent, with flirtation added. When she asks him directly 'Are you single?' she gets the answer that they have been separated for a while, so basically a yes. Okay, it is safe then to continue and engage with the flirtation. Another coffee date happens, and this time it is not for business purposes. A lot of chit-chat ensues, and the waters are being tested. There was also this one odd question about whether the girl gave natural birth. A bit strange, but the conversation flows. The next day, the girl sends the boy a message, only to get the response that he is with his wife, they are still living together (never separate during the apparent separation), and they are working things out. WTF!? In the area where other people noticed their interactions, the girl gets the reputation of being promiscuous. Really? The deceiving boy gets a pat on the back for dodging a bullet, and the deceived girl gets the reputation! Really?

Single moms are viewed as vulnerable and easy targets because they are perceived as unbelievably desperate. When affairs happen (and thank goodness nothing more than an awkward hug happened at this last coffee), the woman usually gets the blame, even more so if she is a single mom. Oh, how the word spreads of the 'easy victim for a fling'. Next thing you know, you become popular, with every second boy you talk to trying his luck for a fling or just a fuck, lining up at your door. Ugh! Fuck off!

On another occasion, the girl is invited to a birthday social event. She is the only single parent, and the evening starts off great. One boy is married, and his wife is home with their new baby. The single mom is well aware of this, and it does not bother her, as she is here to have a good time with friends. She is not looking to be picked up or for any kind of nonsense. But through the night she becomes aware of the boy's eyes on her the whole time, and it becomes uncomfortable. Whenever the other girls leave the table, as things happen at a social, people move around. She would quickly get up and make sure to stay within a group of girls, never to find herself alone. Even though she does not have a best friend there to stick with. During the night's group photo moments, the girl will deliberately push herself into the middle of the other girls, to make sure she does not end up next to the boy.

These are very uncomfortable situations for single moms. We are not looking for trouble. It is not like the single mom puts on a perfume from the bottle labelled 'Go catch the married man'. No! We do not want to be picked up or flirted with by every man we cross paths with. We actually have values and morals. When we are ready to open ourselves up for a relationship, we just want a normal, healthy one. Just because a man looks at us does not mean we invite his attention. There are so many uncalled-for stereotypes.

Let's look at some statistics. Statistics can be manipulated according to what a person is trying to prove. To be objective, I searched the term 'statistics on infidelity' and looked at the first reliable links. All reference links are posted in the reference list:

Discreet Investigations & Security wrote a blog post on a study done between 2010 to 2016, indicating that men (20%) cheat more than women (13%). The study further breaks down different age groups. In the younger age groups, women cheat more, and in the older age groups, men cheat more. It also states that the studies are based on willing participants and thus do not give a clear objective in society.

PsychCentral: in this study done in 2021, they interviewed 441 people, and of these, 46% admitted to cheating. In a second study mentioned in the article, 23% of men cheated and 12% of women. They also say it is difficult to measure cheating as it means different things to different people. Is flirting considered cheating? What about online? Or is it only cheating when there is sex?

Department of Family and Consumer Studies: here they state in the past decade, the number of cheating married men was between 20-25% and married women between 10-15%. They also state that people are more disapproving of cheating now than they were before and that the meaning of marriage has changed.

When searching specifically for married men and single mothers, no studies were found. All the studies look at married men versus married women. This does not excuse the single mother who deliberately gets involved with a married man, knowing he is married. However, many lies are told to women in general by cheating men (and I can assume vice versa). And this is done to lure the person into the affair.

Last month, before I even decided to write this book, I listened to a very interesting video on YouTube by Lisa Bilyeu, who interviewed Dr Ramani. Dr Ramani talks about the type of man who always cheats. As a therapist, she worked with many people and listed categories she created for cheaters. She also explains how people are angrier at the women whom the man cheated with than the actual cheating man. And how people expect better morals from the woman. But she explains that we do not always know the dynamics and what lies were told to the women to draw them into these affairs. The men who cheat are very cunning and skilled at luring a woman in. Thus, it is not so simple to put all the blame on the women who were deceived into an affair. And yes, women should not be naïve. Do your homework. Ask a lot of questions. Do not fall for the flattery and compliments. The dating world today can be daunting.

Some time back I recall reading something on Quora about men dating single mothers. One of the comments said that men liked to date single mothers because they perceived them as nurturing and more open to understanding their circumstances (the sop stories of his unhappy marriage – do not fall for that shit!). Think about it, do you really want to raise another child who needs a mother's nurturing touch?

By no means am I saying to run from every married man. If you find yourself in a social or neighbourly environment, have a chat as long as it is in the group, around the table, close to his wife. But what I do strongly suggest is to avoid being alone with the married man. Whether he has alternative motives or not, it is to avoid people nearby making the wrong assumptions. I think this is just one of those things we need to be very aware of and navigate around. Cheating has happened for decades and will still be a problem for decades to come. But it is one less stress a single mother needs.

Single moms have high values as well. And single moms want good and healthy relationships. Some of us manage to walk the road alone, while others falter at the potential of a partner who promises or creates the illusion of support. Just like many other women, we can make mistakes in choosing the wrong partner. We are not immune to making mistakes. But this does not mean we do not have values and welcome attention from every man who glances in our direction. We are women too, not aliens.

In the study done by Karunanayake, et al. (2021), one participant explained a bizarre moment in her career. She is a teacher, well recognised for being fluent in English, her subject. Another teacher, who happens to be male, sought her help in English. Next thing, the man's wife comes to the school, telling the single mother to stay away from her husband, as she is attempting to take him away from her. She explains how awkward school became as she tried to avoid this fellow teacher at all costs.

Other single mothers in the studies have discussed how they are victimised and threatened by society, which makes the wrong assumptions about them. This causes single mothers to withdraw from society and avoid sharing their emotions, and thoughts with other people.

Perhaps the bottom line is that the wife cannot contain her jealousy in an attempt to keep her marriage together. And the husband cannot keep his straying eyes and desires to himself. If a man wants to cheat, he will cheat, whether it is with the single mother next door or the married woman at work. What I am saying is, that if a man is suspected of cheating, every woman is then a possible suspect, not just the single mother.

But in the end, the single mother is the one who gets demonised.

I want to end this chapter with this funny and relevant meme I saw on social media this week. It said, 'No one is stealing your partner, it's an inside job. Your partner wants to be stolen and they initiated that stealing'.

Let that sink in for a moment...

Ready to Date Again?

You might not be ready to date yet, and that is okay. When you are ready, you can read this chapter again.

Dating when you have children can get tricky. As we saw earlier, some men seem to think a woman with children have extra baggage. But I do think it is still possible to find a good man. Just because some are assholes, doesn't mean they all are. And by no means should you act desperate for love. You will only attract the wrong kind of man, leading to more problems. And let's face it, a single mom does not need more baggage – pun intended. Single moms are seen as vulnerable and easy targets for men who want a woman to look after them. But single moms want a partner, not another child to look after.

He will have to show you that he respects you, values you, and adores you. And if all this is true, this also means he accepts your children. Not just tolerate, but accept them as your focus and become part of your and his life. And this means he does not accept you now and try to change you three months later. No, then that is just manipulation.

It is also important for both of you to have healed from your past. We have all gone through bad experiences. But you cannot bring this into your next relationship. Just keep this in mind, and again, this is not necessarily something you will find out straight away. Even though there are some really good red fags to look out for, which is discussed further below!

Before you decide to open yourself up for a new relationship, first read the book 'Women Who Love Too Much' by Robin Norwood. It is important for you to heal from past relationships and to identify any patterns in your life you need to change. Let's face it, if your past relationship were rosy and solid, you would not be single right now. Thus, be honest with yourself and work on yourself.

Be on the lookout for the guy who is not taking care of his children. And yes, it might be difficult to know at first as he could easily lie about it. But also take a look at how involved he is with his children. And if not, why not? The last thing you want to be is that woman who lives the good life while he is spending a lot of money on you and your children, but does not pay for his own children. Do you really want to be that woman, living the good life at the expense of his earlier children? I suppose some women are more than happy to marry him and build a life together at their expense. As long as her children have everything and more, why would she have a care in the world for the first children? Suppose it is each to their own.

It can be difficult to meet new people. As we have seen, social events can be tricky. Unless your best friend arranged a braai for you to meet the new single dad who moved in next to them, then that is okay. But to avoid getting caught up in love affair nonsense, it is best to stay away and try to avoid situations that can provoke it.

The next best thing is to go to single social events if there are in your area. Or try online dating. I must say, I am not sure how successful online dating is. But I have been there and met some decent men. Some ended in dates, and they ended because our values were different. Let's face it, it takes time to get to know someone. I don't think it is possible to fall in love with someone and know they are the person you want to marry in two months. If it is an arranged marriage, I think those dynamics are different and 'love' is not a requirement.

Here are some red flags in online dating profiles:

1. Photos with Children: Online dating is not the place to showcase your children's faces. While it's fine to mention you have children, displaying them like a showpiece is inappropriate. In my 20s, guys would often borrow a puppy and flaunt it at the mall as a chick magnet. They'd turn to the girls they found most attractive, leaving others like me, who weren't considered pretty, feeling ignored (I was actually looking at the puppy, not the guy).

2. First Photo Alone: If the first photo is a group pic, it's frustrating to guess who he is.

3. Group Photos: Group photos also pose a challenge. They might indicate nervousness about putting oneself out there on dating apps, suggesting a need to hide in the crowd. This can lead to insecurity and the need for constant reassurance in a relationship.

4. Showing Off Wealth: Photos with fancy cars or houses can come across as materialistic. Don't be lured by appearances; the shiny tin is empty inside.

5. Shirtless Photos: A shirtless first photo may indicate insecurity, someone who hides behind their body,

especially if they're flaunting their abs. Conversations might not go beyond the surface level.

6. Filtered Photos: Both women and men should avoid filtered photos. There's no point in hiding behind filters and pretending to look different than you do. Embrace your true self.

7. Drink in Hand: If there's a drink in hand in the first photo, it can give the impression that the person doesn't take themselves seriously and may party excessively. He is probably going to spend more money on alcohol than you.

8. Pet in Every Photo: While pets are wonderful, having them in every photo is not cute. It may suggest an inability to separate his life from his pet. Don't get me wrong. I love pets but I don't need them in every photo to feel better about myself. And I can go to the mall for three hours without worrying about my pet.

9. Little to No Info: Profiles with minimal effort may indicate a lack of seriousness or someone only looking for hookups. Put effort into your profile to attract like-minded individuals.

10. Women in Photos: Avoid photos with other women, especially if they're not family members. This can be off-putting and suggest an inability to maintain boundaries. Especially if it's his mother, as he might be a mama's boy and you'll always be competing with her. Or an overbearing sister.

11. 'Knows How to Treat a Woman': Statements like this are often a red flag because he is talking bullshit if he says he knows how to spoil and treat a woman. If someone truly knew how to treat a woman well, they likely wouldn't be single.

12. Ambiguous Intentions: Profiles that are unclear about what they're looking for may indicate they're only interested in hookups. Look for clarity in their intentions. For example – 'still figuring out', they're just looking for hookups. Or 'friends' - they are probably looking for friends with benefits.

13. Fishing Photos: While fishing may be a hobby, photos of excessive drinking or partying with the boys can be a concern, indicating a potential lifestyle mismatch. Unless you are really into fishing as well.

14. No Photos of Himself: Profiles with no photos of the person, only of pets or objects, may indicate insecurity or a fake profile. Avoid investing time in such profiles.

15. Social Media Photos: If his social media is filled with half-naked or model-type girls, it's a sign of potential distraction and lack of seriousness.

16. Good Quality Photos: Pay attention to the quality of photos. If they're not up to today's standards, they may be old or misleading. With today's cell phone technology, anyone can take a decent photo of themselves. Also, look at the background for clues about his lifestyle and habits.

Here are some red flags to look out for during conversations and at the start of the relationship:

1. Meeting for Coffee or Drink: Some say meeting for coffee or a drink first is a no-no, indicating the person is not taking you seriously and going on multiple cheap dates. However, I believe it's a good way to get to know someone. It's easier to end a short coffee date if things aren't going well, than a longer dinner date. Men tend to expect a kiss after a dinner date. If this is the first time we're meeting face-to-face, there is no way he gets a kiss.

2. Self-Centered Conversations: If he dominates the conversation and talks about himself without showing interest in you, it's a sign of self-centeredness. Healthy conversations involve mutual interest and engagement.

3. Enmeshed Family: On the first date, he should not start talking about his mother or sister. You should be the only woman he is thinking about at that moment. Observe how often he brings up his mother or sister into the conversation, without you asking about them. This could be an indication of enmeshed family bonds, and this is not good. You will have to compete with the mother and sister, and you will NOT win!

4. Negative Talk About Exes: If he constantly badmouths his ex, it could indicate unresolved issues or a lack of respect. It's important to focus on the present and future in a new relationship. You might just be the next ex he is bad-mouthing. If he says all his exes are crazy, he made them crazy. If he says they cheated on him, no, he cheated on them.

5. Financial Prying: If he starts asking too many questions about your finances early in the relationship, like requesting to see your payslip or knowing how much you've saved, it's a red flag. While financial discussions are important, this level of scrutiny is invasive and indicates a lack of boundaries or someone looking for opportunities. Run!

6. Emotional Dumping: If, during pillow talk after your first intimate encounter, he divulges deeply personal and intense information, like a past suicide attempt, it's a sign of emotional blackmail. Such heavy topics are best discussed with a therapist, not a new partner, especially as pillow talk after your first sexual encounter!

7. Avoidance of Simple Dates: If he can't commit to a simple coffee date, it could indicate a lack of interest or willingness to invest time and money in getting to know you. A coffee date is a low-pressure way to meet and see if there's a connection.

8. Pushy Behaviour: If he pressures you to cancel your order during a date, it shows a lack of respect for your choices and boundaries. Walk away if this happens. Yes, the comment 'Are you going to eat that' just as you place an order... he was looking for a cheap date. And it shows controlling behaviour.

9. Relationship with Mother: Pay attention to how he treats his mother, as it can be indicative of how he'll treat you or what he will expect from you. Look for signs of respect and consideration in his interactions with her. But also, take note that the relationship is not enmeshed. You

are not looking for a 'mommy's boy' but also not for a man who does not respect women.

10. The Savior Complex: If he tries to save or rescue you early in the relationship, it could be a sign of controlling behaviour. This type of behaviour often leads to a one-sided and unhealthy dynamic. And ultimately, control.

11. Insecurity and Control: If he questions you about other people you've talked to or met, it shows deep insecurity and potential for controlling behaviour. This can lead to trust issues and unhealthy relationship dynamics.

12. Intuition: Trust your gut. If you feel like he's seeing other people, even if there's no concrete evidence (unless you have great spy skills), it's best to walk away. Your intuition is your most powerful tool in protecting yourself.

13. Gift Giving: If he claims he's not good at buying gifts, it could be an excuse for not putting effort into the relationship. A thoughtful partner will make an effort to understand your preferences and find meaningful gifts. But also, if he keeps showering you with excessive gifts, it can be a form of manipulation and love bombing. No one should buy you a new television after two dates.

14. Treatment of Pets: Pay attention to how he treats his pets, as it can be indicative of his character. If he mistreats or neglects them, it's a red flag. If he cannot go anywhere without them (see point 8 in the previous section)...I don't know, maybe you feel the same about your pets.

15. Respect for Preferences: If he insists on playing music you dislike or disregards your preferences, it shows a lack

of respect for your boundaries. Respect is key to a healthy relationship. I do not want to listen to heavy metal during my Sunday morning brunch.

16. Respect for Your Time: If he expects you to inconvenience yourself, such as driving late at night to pick him up, it shows a lack of consideration for your needs. Setting boundaries is important in these situations. Must I load my children in the car at 11 pm and drive 15 km to pick up his drunk ass because he feels it is the least I can do for him, instead of arranging an Uber for him? No! - see, it is a full sentence.

17. Trust Your Instincts: If something feels off, trust your instincts. You don't need to justify your feelings, and it's okay to walk away from a situation that doesn't feel right, without knowing why it is not right. You will thank yourself later.

18. Family Involvement: If he is reluctant to share information about his family's gift preferences, it could indicate that he's not serious about the relationship, or he is possibly bad-mouthing you to his family. Open communication and consideration for each other's families are important in a healthy relationship.

19. Contributing to the Relationship: If he doesn't contribute to your home or relationship, it's a sign of imbalance. Both partners should contribute in meaningful ways to maintain a healthy relationship. And if he stays over at your place three times a week, he needs to contribute and not treat you like a convenient hotel with an all-you-can-eat buffet.

20. Manipulation: If he tries to make you feel sorry for him, it's a form of manipulation. Healthy relationships are based on mutual respect, not guilt or pity. And sometimes it can be the wildest of stories. Sometimes it is a story of how his wife died and he is looking after their children, looking for pity. Or his ex-wife is a drug addict. Or his father just died, just as you started withdrawing on communication. Or if he tries to manipulate you with sexual jokes or remarks about your body early in the relationship, it's a red flag. No one will tell me whether I am allowed to wear black eyeliner or not. Healthy relationships are based on mutual respect, not manipulation. Or if he ever asks 'What am I getting in return' for instance when you ask him something, not like for money or anything but when he feels entitled to get something in return. That man is super transactional and nothing he ever gives you will be 'free and just because he is nice'.

21. Avoiding Comparison: If he compares you to his ex, it shows a lack of respect for your individuality. Each person and relationship is unique, and comparisons are unfair. This could be a possible indication of the need to control you, or he is still dealing with his previous breakup trauma.

22. False Representations: If he portrays himself as someone he's not, such as claiming to have a successful business, it's a red flag. Honesty and transparency are essential in a healthy relationship. On this topic, a very important note. This is often an online scam with fake businesses and 'great investment opportunities' that they later present to you, once you are emotionally hooked in. There have been several reports of fake business setups, with websites to make it look legit. But you are only going to lose your 'investment' as his actual job title is Scammer.

23. Meet Face to Face!: There have been many reports of women being scammed out of their money. The relationship unfolds online and the love bombing happens, and things are rosy. But he cannot see you tomorrow because he needs to travel to you, and his money is tied up. It sounds silly to write this up, but it has happened in far more detail to so many vulnerable women, who 'lend' him the money, which he promises to give back as soon as he arrives, just to never get it back and eventually he disappears. Do not give money! The minute he asks for a dime or dollar, block and run! And be careful with the online chat where there are a lot of spelling errors. He is probably from another country looking for his next scam victim. And with the scammers, you never meet, for all, we know it could be a woman and it is her full-time job to scam lonely and desperate people.

24. Consistency: Pay attention to how consistent he is in his communication and actions. Inconsistencies can be a sign of dishonesty or lack of genuine interest. And does his online profile stay the same, or is he often making changes to it?

25. Safety Precautions: Always meet in a public place and use your own transportation to ensure your safety. It's important to prioritise your well-being in any new relationship.

26. Do some PI work: At some point, hopefully, before you get too deep into the relationship, internet 'stalk' him to find out more or to even see if there is a wife (not an ex like he is proclaiming). Try to do some homework. It is okay, and he is probably doing the same to you. And if he

and his wife are divorced but he has not removed all their photos, like wedding pics or snuggled up...uhm. Ya. There can be several explanations but most of them are not good for you. Let him go!

27. Setting Boundaries: If he crosses your boundaries or tries to pressure you into doing things you're not comfortable with, it's a sign of disrespect. Healthy relationships are built on mutual respect for each other's boundaries. If he did something and you called him out and he said 'I'm sorry YOU feel that way' and doesn't elaborate why he is sorry or at least give a solution or say he won't do it again. He isn't taking accountability; his apology is ingenuine, and he doesn't believe he is in the wrong.

28. Respecting Personal Space: If he doesn't respect your personal space or boundaries, it's a sign of disrespect. It's important to establish and maintain boundaries in any relationship. Like late-night texting and irregular texting for days. It is probably a sign that he is not that interested or has someone already.

29. Avoiding High-Pressure Situations: If he pressures you into sexual activities or asks for intimate photos early in the relationship, it's a sign of disrespect and manipulation. Trust your instincts and prioritise your dignity. Do Not send naked pics. And if he sends you one, block him!

30. Love Bombing: When he is constantly and frequently messaging you, to try to keep you under his spell. And apparently, if he asks you on a date within the first week - massive red flag - don't go and don't continue the

conversations. Either he is very desperate or he is going to love bomb the hell out of you.

31. Continuous Compliments: This is typical narcissistic behaviour to try to flatter and charm you. Stay away!

32. Double Messaging Sending: When you don't respond soon enough, or he follows it up with 'What are you busy with? Why aren't you replying or am I not good enough for you anymore?' Or even asks if he did something wrong. Playing the victim in any shape or form is a massive red flag - narcissistic behaviour and super clingy and insecure behaviour.

33. Trust in a Relationship is Important: If he is trustworthy and reliable, it's a positive sign for a healthy relationship. Trust is essential for a strong and lasting connection. But if he is hiding something, for example, he always puts his phone face down (so that the camera does not scratch, is a crap excuse)? Is he getting notifications and calls? Does he respond to messages? If yes... he is not that into you. Or if he already started calling you pet names without being serious or committed. He is scared to mess up names and probably goes on multiple dates too.

34. How He Treats Others: Watch how he treats others around him, especially those below him. Watch how he treats women who aren't interested in him. His behaviour will tell you a lot. Is he always friendly with everyone? Or does he treat the waiters as less? That's how he will treat you the moment you displease him or upset him. Look how he treats his mother or talks to her on the phone. And does he always expect her to pay or does he pay for lunch when he is out with his mother?

35. Stability: Never fall for a guy who does not have a job. You will just end up with extra weight to carry and drama. Look for someone stable. You are not looking to be a gold digger, but you need stability in your life. Not dead weight. And do not just believe everything he says. People tell you what they want you to hear, not the truth. It is a human thing, we all do it. Ironically, if he mentions anything about gold diggers, then he is probably broke. Just a side note.

36. Fairytales: If he is building castles in the sky and start saying things like 'in 6 months I will be here or my business will achieve this in the next year', he is talking shit and is probably not planning to hang around that long. Or if he starts telling you the fairytales of how you two are going to ride the sunset in road trips you two will take in a custom-built camping van... either he is delusional or starting to love bomb you to give him lots of your money. Let's be realistic, how many people build these fairytales within the first 6 months of meeting someone? It is not normal healthy behaviour... they are working on a plan here.

37. Body Count: It first starts with him wanting to know how many people you are talking to while you two are still sussing things out. Then later he wants to know how many relationships you have had and how many people you slept with. He is studying you, to manipulate you and to see what you think your worth is. If he asks this, you tell him how good you were treated (even if it is a lie) and then end it and move on with your life.

38. His Lifestyle: Does he still live with his parents? Sorry to say, but he is never going to take you seriously. Is he a gamer? They are going to spend all their time gaming and

neglect you. Does he bring his dogs up in the conversation? It is an odd one but he is either looking for a partner who is loyal like a dog or he is trying to get attention. Note: the dog thing keeps coming up.

39. Character Traits: If he is looking for independent women, he wants you to take care of him. If it is ambition, he is not going to invest in you as you are able to provide for yourself. If he wants to 'build' with you, he is looking for a housewife he can take for granted and you will end up sacrificing your bare bones for him.

40. And lastly, do NOT have sex on the first date! Neuroscientist, Dr. Tara Swart, explained when heterosexual couples get to know each other, the woman's oxytocin levels increase slowly during dating. Still, during an orgasm it increases vastly, creating a stronger bond with her partner. If a man has sex on the first date his vasopressin levels drop and testosterone takes over. If he has to wait for sex, his vasopressin and oxytocin levels increase slowly over time, and by the time he has sex with his partner, he is already bonded. It is just science – make him wait!

It is a lot, I know. But the most important thing to remember is not to be desperate. Make him work for your attention! If he ends up ignoring you, then so be it. There are other fish in the sea. I am not sure how 'plentiful' it is but rather wait a little longer for a decent man (not perfect because they don't exist. Be realistic) instead of settling for crap because you felt desperate or lonely. Take your time to get to know him. And it is okay if you don't like him or he does not like you. Make an effort to dress up for your dates. And if he did not ask you out within three weeks, then he is not really into you or he is living abroad and a professional scammer. Either way, it is okay. Accept it and move on.

Lessons Learned

One of the first things I learned was how to be comfortable in my own space. Some people struggle with solitude; they cannot function alone. Even though I grew up as an only child, I still had to learn this comfort. Loneliness can be suffocating, but it also offers a great space for self-reflection and goal setting. Often, our friends and family, fearing our failure, may trample on our dreams. However, sometimes we need to keep these dreams and desires to ourselves for a while, nurturing them like a delicate seedling. Only once strong enough, do we share these dreams. Don't hesitate to dream and work to turn those dreams into reality. Whether it is to start studying, start a small business, or take that special trip. Like a little seedling, we can share these dreams once it is strong enough to be repotted. Don't be afraid to dream and work to turn those dreams into reality.

Another great lesson was honesty with myself and accepting things as they are. There are many aspects of life we can change, but far more that we cannot. Learning to accept reality may sound simple (as we assume it comes naturally), but it requires conscious practice to let go of unchangeable circumstances.

In 2019, I faced a stressful divorce, financial struggles, and a traumatic hijacking. As a photographer, I knew that without work, there would be no income and I was concerned for my children's wellbeing. Thus, falling ill or having a nervous breakdown was not an option! At the time, I did go to therapy to cope with the stress. During therapy, I expressed concerns about potentially breaking down. My therapist, after a few probing questions, calmly reassured me that she did not foresee a breakdown. She explained that this was because I naturally accepted things as they were and did not suppress my emotions. This approach, I realised, was not only normal but mentally healthy—almost like a superpower. Since then, I sometimes felt it was like my superpower.

What does it mean to accept things as they are? Consider the Serenity Prayer, which many know from various sources: *'God, grant me the serenity to accept the things I cannot change, the courage to change the things I can, and the wisdom to know the difference.'* When possible, we act to change outcomes, like removing a stubborn stain rather than buying a new shirt. However, we must also recognise the limits of our control, such as accepting temporary inconveniences like a burst water pipe causing your complex to have no water for days, or societal stigmas on single mothers. I hope this book offers some perspective and inspires a bit of change.

I also learned about the importance of a growth mindset, which involves believing that our abilities, intelligence, and talents can develop through dedication, hard work, and learning. People with a growth mindset embrace challenges, persist through setbacks, view failures as growth opportunities, and understand that their potential is not fixed but can be cultivated through continuous learning and effort. Inspired by Carol Dweck's TED talk, which popularised this concept, I recommend watching her enlightening presentation, linked in the reference list. She popularized the growth mindset, contrasting it with a fixed mindset—the belief that abilities and intelligence are innate and unchangeable. A growth mindset encourages resilience, a love for learning, and a willingness to take risks, all of which are beneficial for personal development and success in various aspects of life.

Another critical lesson was the necessity to eliminate debt, especially crucial for single mothers. Debt restricts your freedom, feeling like a noose around your neck. Facing financial realities head-on is vital, regardless of your current financial situation. Two enlightening books on this topic are Manage Your Money Like a Grownup by Sam Beckbessinger and The Psychology of Money by Morgan Housel.

Please do not be scared to face this thing called money. If you feel you don't have any money left to work with, then that is the exact reason to read the books and see where you can start. As much as I am 'preaching' right now, I too am still a work-in-progress to manage my money instead of letting it drag me by the nose like a bull with one of those steel rings through its nose.

Two other insightful books I recommend reading are 'The Art of Possibility by Rosamund Stone Zander and Benjamin Zander, and A New Earth by Eckhart Tolle. I have learned from these books how to be present in the moment, as well as overcoming adversities. Living in the past draws us away from the now, and then we are not able to take the steps we need to take to make the desired changes in our present. One thing you need to realise is that your brain does not know the difference between what you are thinking about and what you are experiencing. If you keep thinking about how things are going wrong, your brain perceives it as real and causes your body to act accordingly, putting you in survival mode (alerting your sympathetic nervous system). This is a very oversimplified explanation. But the point I am trying to make is the importance of managing your thoughts, and I found that living in the moment helps a great deal with that! If you are struggling with stress and survival mode, another great book to read is 'Thrive' by Richard Sutton. The book is based on his knowledge of the sports industry, but resilience applies to everyone. Learn how to grow, maintain and appreciate the strong resilience you have built up. Live in the moment, dream about the future and learn from the past. But do not stay in the past or too far ahead in the future. The now is what counts.

I also learned to be resourceful. Whether it's preparing meals from scraps or enjoying outings on a budget (by taking water bottles from home instead of buying coldrinks), it's possible to live well with less. And for most parts (if you can avoid buying gluten-free products) we eat fairly healthy on a low budget. Ironically, the 'fast' and convenient stuff is often the pricey and unhealthy stuff. Those easy meals do save time, I get it. Next time you cook rice, make a double portion and freeze the other portion. When you are making a braai at home and you know only half the garlic roll will be enjoyed, split it and freeze the other half for next time. And like I have explained before, with a little non-fancy hand stitching and a few buttons, you can make something old and second-hand look great again. It is possible to make things work with what you have.

This reminds me of after the divorce. I found a two-bedroom flat for my children and myself, and we moved in with the bare minimum. Everything I owned could fit inside the back of a bakkie with a small trailer, the length of a double bed, and two carloads of clothing, bedding, and some kitchen stuff. I went to the lowest-priced shop to buy a broom and mop and the cheapest curtains I could find. For a month, my children were 'camping' in their shared room on mattresses before I finally found them two single beds I could afford. I did have to drive about 60km to pick up the unassembled beds and it took me an hour or two to assemble them myself. Slowly, we built up our new home from scratch.

For months, I could not have visitors because the lounge area was so empty my children used it as their scooter park and everything echoed in this part of the flat. Looking back, these are fun memories, and our home has grown a lot since then - a testament to our growth and resilience.

The day I moved out of that flat, I was astonished by how much our lives grew. When the mover arrived with the big truck, I think it was a 20-foot truck, I recall thinking 'How many flats is he moving together'. But the truck kept filling up with my stuff. It was a proud moment to compare how our lives changed, from when we first moved into that flat. And still today, most of my furniture is second-hand, and I have a beautiful and neatly styled home.

Maintaining health is crucial amidst life's challenges. When you have your whole life in order but your health is failing, then I think everything else does not matter. Between all the juggling and ups and downs, please take care of your health. Even if the only exercise you get to do is 15 minutes of half-asleep yoga at night before you crawl into bed, then do it. Or go for a walk at your local Park Run every Saturday morning. Take your children with you.

There are plenty of people with their children either walking or toddlers in a stroller. You can even take your dog with you if you have one.

Also, take care of what you eat, because this has a big impact on our health. Sugar is as big a demon as debt! I know that secret chocolate at night brings so much bliss. But it can cause bigger problems down the line. I was told a boiled egg helps to manage the sugar cravings and it seems to work for me. Another trick is flavoured tea. Try some different flavours, there are several delicious teas. One of my favourites is Peach and Apricot Rooibos tea.

And this goes for sleep as well. When our babies are just a few months old, we can cope with the lack of sleep for a short period. However, our bodies are not built to endure prolonged sleep deprivation. If you suffer from insomnia, it's important to seek help and research sleep health. A prominent advocate for understanding sleep is Dr. Andrew Huberman, a neuroscientist with a YouTube channel. He discusses research and interviews other experts to share valuable public insights. I recommend listening to his channel and exploring one of his many podcasts on sleep. Although they can be lengthy, you have the option to listen at a faster speed or skip less relevant sections. The more you listen, the more you'll grasp the underlying concepts, even if the terminology seems complex at first.

Sleep deprivation has significant impacts on mental health and physical functions, such as insulin regulation, and can even contribute to depression. From personal experience, listening to such podcasts has been incredibly educational.

Lastly, the saying 'It takes a village to raise a child' rings true. Some women have a strong support network, while others may find it more challenging to cultivate. It can be particularly tough to build this network as a single mother when social opportunities like playdates may be scarce. However, wherever possible, try to strengthen your support system by reaching out to friends, family, and community resources. Consider employing a nanny to care for your children every other Saturday, allowing you some much-needed personal time.

Life doesn't have to be perfect to be enjoyable. On particularly tough days, an extra cup of coffee can make all the difference.

In Closing

In South Africa, about half of the women with children are single mothers, and shockingly, only about 12% of divorced fathers pay maintenance. Yes, just 12%! To any man reading this book who falls into that category of 12%, you deserve a fucking medal!! Your support for your children is commendable regardless of your feelings towards your ex-wife, girlfriend, fiancée, or partner.

Sadly, these statistics are outdated and based on, what seems to be the last recorded statistics in South Africa, in 2015/16! After several searches, newer statistics could not be found. The South African Law is well set out on paper and to some extent, the 'simpler' cases get resolved, even though it can take months. The simple fact is that the courts are flooded daily with people seeking assistance, creating backlogs and a poorly implemented Law. All a man needs to do is to immigrate (AKA – run away) to a country with no reciprocal order and he lives a free life not needing to spend another cent on his children and leaving their mom to deal with it all. Oh, and Public Schooling in South Africa is not free.

Women, whether single or not, face numerous systemic challenges. Even considering income disparities, as highlighted in a book I'm currently reading, women typically earn about 30% less than men—a global issue. This book also explores reasons such as gendered job assignments, perceived competence, and the sacrifices women often make for family care.

I strongly recommend Manage Your Money Like a Fucking Grownup by Sam Beckbessinger to all women, irrespective of marital or parental status. It's crucial to understand financial management, especially for women, and this is why I'm mentioning this resource for the second time in this book.

Every morning, we rise, put on our best smiles, and take on the world one step at a time. Behind these smiles, we all harbour our struggles, which makes it pointless to dwell on them incessantly. Appreciating what we have can be tough, especially when overshadowed by our needs. Being a single mother is a challenging journey, and having been married before, I've experienced both realms of raising children. My narrative, rooted in the perspective of a single mom, does not diminish the experiences of married mothers or those with active partners.

The difficulties of single parenthood often go unnoticed because we seldom discuss them. We've been so stigmatised and stereotyped, and I hope this book helps shatter at least some of those misconceptions. Often, even when single mothers socialise, we skirt around these societal stereotypes, perhaps because we've resigned ourselves to them. But should we just accept them? We work incredibly fucking hard to provide for and raise our children without needing the additional societal stress. This solidarity is likely why single mothers often band together—we need to support each other in the absence of broader societal support, even amidst our own chaos.

A message to single moms:
There are unspoken rules and unfair treatments we've come to accept. Yet, perhaps the single mother is stronger than she realises, possibly even intimidating others with her resilience. Single moms, stand tall! You carry a heavier

burden yet continue to persevere. Do not let societal views diminish you. Stand up, dust yourself off, fix your crown, and stand firm. You are equipped to raise your children.

From Carl Jung's The Red Book: 'Embrace the chaos. There is magic in chaos. Love is the unification of opposites and, essentially, love is magic'.

References

Beckbessinger, S. (2018). Manage your Money like a fucking Grownup, Jonothan Ball Publishers.

Bilyeu, L., & Ramani, D. (Bilyeu, L). (2023, December 20). This Type of Man Always Cheats!, Womand of Impact Podcast. Retrieved from https://www.youtube.com/watch?v=ydNz1pZd-z0

Bock, J. D. (2000). Doing the right thing? Gender & Society, 14(1), 62–86.

Burnett Attorneys & Notaries Inc, Enforcing Foreign Maintenance Orders, 17 Aug 2023, https://www.burnett-law.co.za/enforcing-foreign-maintenance-orders/

Daily Maverick. (2023, October 12). SARS could be the vital answer in fixing South Africa's broken child maintenance system. Retrieved from https://www.dailymaverick.co.za/article/2023-10-12-sars-could-be-the-vital-answer-in-fixing-south-africas-broken-child-maintenance-system/

Department of Family & Consumer Studies. (n.d.). Infidelity (Wolfinger). University of Utah. Retrieved from https://fcs.utah.edu/news/infidelity-wolfinger.php

Discreet Investigations & Security. (n.d.). Infidelity statistics: Who cheats more, men or women? Discreet Investigations & Security Blog. Retrieved from https://discreetinvestigations.ca/infidelity-statistics-who-cheats-more-men-or-women/

Dweck, C. (2014, October 9), Developing a Growth Mindset with Carol Dweck. https://www.youtube.com/watch?v=hiiEeMN7vbQ

Hopper, E. (2020, February 24). Maslow's Hierarchy of Needs Explained. *Thought Co.* https://www.thoughtco.com/maslows-hierarchy-of-needs-4582571

Howes, L. (2023, June 22). We attract people based on psychological wounds" #1 neuroscientist explains how to manifest love! YouTube. https://www.youtube.com/watch?v=lzvE0Z-g5m4

Huberman, A. Youtube channel: https://www.youtube.com/c/AndrewHubermanLab

Ivy Panda. (n.d.). How does society view single parents? IvyPanda. Retrieved from https://ivypanda.com/essays/single-parents-and-society/

Gneezy, U., Leonard, K. L., & List, J. A. (2006). Gender differences in competition: The role of socialization. Manuscript, University of Chicago.

Karunanayake, D. D. K. S., Aysha, M. N., & Vimukthi, N. D. U. (2021). The psychological well-being of single mothers with school age children: An exploratory study. Int. J. Sci. Res. Sci. Technol, 8, 16-37.

Maslow, A. H. (1943). A theory of human motivation. Psychological Review, 50, 370 -396. https://psychclassics.yorku.ca/Maslow/motivation.htm

News24, 28 Nov 2019, Meet the single mom shining a spotlight on child maintenance and financial abuse issues in South Africa, https://www.news24.com/life/archive/meet-the-single-mom-shining-a-spotlight-on-child-maintenance-and-financial-abuse-issues-in-south-africa-20191128

NNEDV, About Financial Abuse, https://nnedv.org/content/about-financial-abuse/

PsychCentral. (n.d.). How common is cheating (infidelity), really? PsychCentral Blog. Retrieved from https://psychcentral.com/blog/how-common-is-cheating-infidelity-really#statistics

Ricotta, J., & Marks, K. (n.d.). What is workplace discrimination against single mothers? Queens Employment Attorney. Retrieved from https://www.queensemploymentattorney.com/faq/what-is-workplace-discrimination-against-single-mothers/

Rusyda, H. M., Lukman, Z. M., Subhi, N., Chong, S. T., Latiff, A. A., Hasrul, H., & Amizah, W. W. (2011). Coping with difficulties: Social inequality and stigmatization on single mothers with low-income household. Pertanika J. Social Sciences & Humanities, 19, 157-162.

Schein, V. E. (2001). A global look at psychological barriers to women's progress in management. Journal of Social Issues, 57(4), 675-688.

Stack, R. J., & Meredith, A. (2018). The Impact of Financial Hardship on Single Parents: An Exploration of the Journey From Social Distress to Seeking Help. Journal of Family and Economic Issues, 39(4), DOI:10.1007/s10834-017-9551-6

Statistics South Africa. (2022). Marriages and Divorces 2022. Retrieved from https://www.statssa.gov.za/publications/P0318/P03182022.pdf

Torres-Mackie, N. (2020). Cultivating Capacities: How Children of Single Mothers Manage Stigma and Endure Strain (Doctoral dissertation, Columbia University).

Wire, what is financial Abuse, https://www.wire.org.au/financial-abuse/

Other Books Mentioned in this Book

Here is the list of books and their authors I talked about in this book, and suggested you read:

- Women Who Love To Much by Robin Norwood
- Thrive – the Power of Resilience by Richard Sutton
- The Art of Possibility by Rosamund Stone Zander and Benjamin Zander
- A New Earth – Create a Better Life by Eckhart Tolle
- Manage your Money like a Grownup by Sam Beckbessinger
- The Psychology of Money by Morgan Housel

For more great book suggestions, take a look at my website at
www.monya.co.za

About the Author

Monya Maxwell is a passionate advocate for personal development and mental wellness, blending her background in photography with her studies in counselling and psychology to create a unique approach to mindfulness and self-discovery. With over eight years of experience as a newborn and maternity photographer, she understands the importance of capturing life's fleeting moments and cherishing the journey of motherhood.

Driven by a desire to empower single mothers and raise awareness about issues such as financial abuse, Monya Maxwell is currently working on her book, 'Shits and Giggles - Diaries of a Solo Mom,' which explores the challenges and triumphs of single motherhood with humour and candor. Through her writing, she aims to inspire others to embrace their strengths, find joy in everyday moments, and navigate life's ups and downs with resilience and grace.

*We are meant to grow,
so we have something to give.*

Find out more about Monya - www.monya.co.za

Shits and Giggles – Screw Burnout!
Burnout doesn't have to be the end of your story—it can be the beginning of your biggest transformation. Shits and Giggles – Screw Burnout! takes you on a humorous, no-nonsense journey to understand and conquer burnout. Monya Maxwell offers practical tools, real-life insights, and a hefty dose of self-compassion to help you reclaim your spark, refuel your energy, and get back to living the life you deserve. Say goodbye to burnout and hello to your comeback. It's time to put yourself first—no guilt, no shame.

Closing the Book – The Art of Emotional Evolution
This deeply personal visual and written journey explores the emotional terrain of healing, self-discovery, and letting go. Closing the Book is not a story of victimhood, but a testament to resilience—the courage it takes to face your pain, do the inner work, and step into your own light. Through evocative imagery and heartfelt reflections, Monya invites readers to witness a quiet yet powerful transformation: from holding on to finally letting go.

Coming soon.

www.ingramcontent.com/pod-product-compliance
Lightning Source LLC
Chambersburg PA
CBHW072010290426
44109CB00018B/2199